VIKING SOCIETY FOR NORTHERN RESEARCH
TEXT SERIES

GENERAL EDITORS
Alison Finlay and Carl Phelpstead

VOLUME XXI

THE SAGA OF BISHOP THORLAK

(ÞORLÁKS SAGA BYSKUPS)

The printing of this book is made possible by a gift to the University of Cambridge in memory of Dorothea Coke, Skjaeret, 1951.

THE SAGA OF BISHOP THORLAK

ÞORLÁKS SAGA BYSKUPS

TRANSLATED BY ÁRMANN JAKOBSSON
AND DAVID CLARK

VIKING SOCIETY FOR NORTHERN RESEARCH
UNIVERSITY COLLEGE LONDON
2013

© Ármann Jakobsson and David Clark
ISBN: 978-0-903521-88-8

Cover image: Saint Þorlákr. Image from the Hólar altar cloth, fifteenth century. Property of the National Museum of Iceland.

Printed by Short Run Press Limited, Exeter

CONTENTS

INTRODUCTION	vii
TRANSLATION	1
NOTES	33
BIBLIOGRAPHY AND ABBREVIATIONS	51
INDEX OF PERSONAL NAMES	63
INDEX OF PLACE NAMES	65

ACKNOWLEDGEMENTS

The authors wish to thank Viðar Pálsson for his assistance with the Introduction and the Þjóðminjasafn Íslands (National Museum of Iceland) for permission to reproduce the image of Bishop Þorlákr from the Hólar altar cloth.

INTRODUCTION

1

The translation of St Þorlákr's remains on 20 July 1198 was an important event not just in the history of one saint but also in the history of Icelandic literature, since his translation and subsequent veneration mark the beginning of indigenous hagiography in Iceland. Bjarni Aðalbjarnarson remarked in 1958 that the translation of Þorlákr in 1198 was the main prerequisite for the ensuing biographies of the saint (Bjarni Aðalbjarnarson 1958, 35–37).[1] First comes religious veneration; the literature follows.

And so it did, quite swiftly. The Oldest Book of Miracles (*Jarteinabók elzta*) is believed to be almost contemporaneous with Þorlákr's translation, since it exists in a manuscript dated to the first quarter of the thirteenth century.[2] It is hard to find an Icelandic manuscript that is closer both to the original text and to the events depicted. The manuscripts of the oldest saga of Þorlákr (the A-version of the saga), the text translated in this volume, are younger, but it is generally accepted that it was probably composed in the first decade of the thirteenth century, before the death of his successor, Bishop Páll Jónsson, in 1211.[3] This was followed by a younger version

---

[1] The content of Bjarni's article was anticipated in Einar Ól. Sveinsson 1954, 8–9.

[2] It is preserved as the earliest section of AM 645 4to, dated to *c*.1220. Despite evident losses it includes forty-six miracles from shortly after Þorlákr's translation to March 1200. Its core must be the set of miracles written down on Bishop Páll Jónsson's initiative and read at the Alþingi in summer 1199, hence its alias *Jarteinabók Páls biskups* (*Jarteinabók Þorláks byskups in forna*). The three surviving versions of the saga of St Þorlákr (known as A, B, and C) contain variously overlapping miracle collections, the A- and B-versions in single manuscripts (*c*.1360 and early fourteenth century respectively) while the C-version's collection has a more complex tradition (fourteenth-century to seventeenth-century manuscripts), and could conceivably have originated as two separate collections. For an overview see Ásdís Egilsdóttir 2002, xxxii, c; cf. *Ordbog*, 3 412.

[3] Guðbrandur Vigfússon and Finnur Jónsson believed *Þorláks saga* dovetailed with *Hungrvaka*, which they judged to have been put down either between *c*.1200 and Páll's death in 1211 (Finnur) or after the death of Gizurr Hallsson in 1206 and before Páll's in 1211 (Guðbrandur) (Guðbrandur Vigfússon 1858, xxxi–xxxiv (where he refutes his earlier dating of *Þorláks saga* to 1198, cf. 331 n.); Finnur Jónsson 1920–24, II 566). Sigurður Nordal likewise assigned both sagas to 1206–11, primarily on grounds of his 'three school' model of saga composition which saw *Hungrvaka* and *Þorláks saga* as influenced by *Jóns saga helga* and the Þingeyrar

(the B-version) in the late thirteenth century and yet another with more miracles (the C-version) in the fourteenth century (see section 4 below). The translation of Þorlákr's remains is described in several versions of the Þorlákr legend. Here is the A-version's account (see ch. 82):

> It was agreed among all the leading men in the land, clerical and lay, to take his body out of the earth. Therefore Bishop Páll called together clerics and chieftains to Skálaholt. First there was Bishop Brandr from Hólar, Priest Guðmundr Arason, who later was bishop, Sæmundr and Ormr, brothers of Bishop Páll, Hallr and Þorvaldr and Magnús Gizurarson, Þorleifr from Hítardalr and many other chieftains. There was great flooding of the rivers at that time throughout the whole land, but God wished that that impede no man from travelling to the see. And when they had all come together they all kept vigil during the night, to the praise of God and the holy Þorlákr.
>
> During the following day his holy relics were taken out of the earth and carried into the church with hymns and songs of praise and beautiful processions and with all the honour and veneration which could be achieved in this land. The coffin was set down in the choir and clerics then sang the *Te Deum*, and sick men knelt at the coffin and many men were healed thereby.

It is evident from this narrative that the veneration of Þorlákr had the approval of the Icelandic élite. Their presence in Skálaholt on this day makes clear the official nature of the event.[4] Although all existing narrative

---

school (1933, lxii–lxviii). Similarly, Jón Helgason judged *Jóns saga helga* older than *Þorláks saga* (1934, 192). Bjarni Aðalbjarnarson (1958), followed by Jakob Benediktsson (1969, esp. 106–07), saw the issue as essentially ecclesiastical, and linked the production of texts on Þorlákr directly to his translation. Neither *Hungrvaka* nor *Jóns saga helga* is now considered older than *Þorláks saga*, itself dated closer to 1200 and thought to be the oldest of the *biskupa sögur*. Another blow to the theory of Þingeyrar's leadership in the field was Ólafía Einarsdóttir's powerful objection (1964, 127–42) to previous interpretations of early Icelandic uses of the Gerlandic calendar (*computatio Gerlandi*), drawn on by Nordal (1952, 212–14) and laid out most fully by Jón Jóhannesson (1952). See Ásdís Egilsdóttir 2002, xxiv–xxxi, lii, cix–cx.

[4] Until the early thirteenth century sainthood was commonly declared through either regional councils or episcopal powers. From the end of the tenth century, and increasingly in the eleventh and the twelfth, it became common to seek the presence of the pope (or his legate) at the declaration, for added prestige and recognition. The papacy successfully turned custom into preconditioning rule, and by the pontificate of Alexander III (1159–81) papal approval had become *de facto* indispensable. Lateran IV proclaimed the making of saints a papal prerogative, but it was only in 1234 that declaration of sainthood became fully *de jure* a papal act, by which the pope entered saints into the official canon (hence *canonisation*, emerging as a legal term no earlier than the early eleventh century). Practically all early Norse saints, including

sources about St Þorlákr stress the presence of the most distinguished people of Iceland, however, they also emphasise that of the nameless poor. St Þorlákr not only aids the abbot of Þykkvabœr and his successor's brother-in-law in getting their health back, he also helps a nameless poor man find a lost piece of string and a poor farmer's wife club a seal so that her family can survive the Icelandic winter. Thus the cult of the saint became something in which rich and poor could share.[5]

2

Religious writing in Iceland is believed to have started with the advent and institutionalisation of Christianity in the early eleventh century. Both the *Íslendingabók* of Ari inn fróði 'the Learned' (c.1125) and *Hungrvaka* (c.1200) mention the visits of foreign bishops in the eleventh century who presumably brought learning with them,[6] and the See of Skálaholt

---

Þorlákr, were declared through episcopal powers alone. Summoning the clerical and lay *optimates* to Skálaholt for the event no doubt helped ensure its legitimacy, even if it conformed to custom and, strictly speaking, did not violate canon law. Jón Helgason suggested that the Latin *vita* may have been written in order to win papal approval, but there is little to substantiate this (1976, 389; for a sceptical response, see Ásdís Egilsdóttir 2002, cx). For international and ecclesiastical contexts of the event see Vauchez 1988, Heinzelmann 1979, Schlafke 1960, Kemp 1948, Weinstein and Bell 1982.

[5] The social and economic transformations of the central Middle Ages brought to the fore and intensified links between the holy and *pauperes*, a term encompassing not only the poor but the powerless in general. One manifestation was the growing cult of St Nicholas of Myra, fuelled by his traditional reputation as a protector of the poor and powerless as well as by the theft of his relics and their translation to Bari (ON Bár) in Italy in 1087. His reputation spread speedily, his *vita* had already been translated into Norse by the twelfth century, and the author of *Hungrvaka* (22) saw reason to point out that St Nicholas was translated in the days of Bishop Gizurr. Gizurr Hallsson himself arrives from Bár at a crucial moment later in the text (35), apparently to his great prestige. Thus St Þorlákr, friend of *potentes* and *pauperes*, fits the international context well, and he (or his sanctified reconstruction) was obviously informed by that context. On high medieval social and economic transformations, social terms, and saints and their miracles see Moore 2000, esp. 19–64. On St Nicholas and his cult see Meisen 1931; Blöndal 1949; Widding 1961a; 1961b; Sverrir Tómasson 1982; Gad 1967.

[6] Ari speaks of the missionary priests Þangbrandr, sent by King Óláfr Tryggvason, and Þormóðr. Þangbrandr's mission is reported most fully in *Óláfs saga Tryggvasonar en mesta* (1958–2000, I 149–50, 168, 221, II 64–66, 150–61, 163–66), *Kristni saga* (13–29) and *Brennu-Njáls saga* (1954, 256–69), where he is variously said to be

was established with the consecration of the Westphalia-educated Ísleifr Gizurarson as bishop in 1056 (*Hungrvaka*, 6).[7] In his lifetime Skálaholt was not the bishop's official residence; it belonged to his family and he used it as his abode. It is with the election of his son Gizurr in his father's place in 1082 that Skálaholt gains its official status and, after his death, succeeding bishops of Skálaholt lived there, of whom Þorlákr was the sixth (*Íslendingabók*, 22–23, *Hungrvaka*, 8, 16).[8] After 1106 their domain encompassed only the south, west and east of Iceland as the North had its own bishop at Hólar (*Íslendingabók*, 23; *Hungrvaka*, 17–18; *Jóns saga ins helga*, 193–202).[9] In Þorlákr's day that diocese was held by Brandr Sæmundarson (1163–1201) who later played a major role in Þorlákr's elevation to sanctity, as well as

---

Saxon, Flemish or from Bremen; he is called Þorbrandr in the Þórðarbók redaction of *Landnámabók* (348–49). On these conversion narratives, see e.g. Grønlie 2005. The nationality of Þormóðr, who is otherwise referred to only later in *Kristni saga* (31) and as Thermo in Theodoricus's Latin history of Norway (*HN*, 21), is obscure. Ari gives a catalogue of twelve missionary bishops: 'Friðrekr kom í heiðni hér, en þessir váru síðan: Bjarnharðr enn bókvísi fimm ár, Kolr fá ár. Hróðolfr nítján ár, Jóhan enn írski fá ár, Bjarnharðr nítján ár, Heinrekr tvau ár. Enn kvómu hér aðrir fimm, þeir es byskupar kváðusk vesa: Ǫrnolfr ok Goðiskolkr ok þrír ermskir: Petrus ok Abrahám ok Stephánus' (*Íslendingabók* 18; see also 14–15, 21). *Hungrvaka* (8–9, 11–13) names Kolr, Friðrekr, Jón inn írski, Bjarnvarðr bókvísi, Rúðolfr or Úlfr, Heinrekr and Bjarnvarðr inn saxlenzki. Kolr appears widely as Kollr Víkverjabiskup, Jóhan and Jón are one and the same, as are Bjarnharðr and Bjarnvarðr, and Hróðolfr and Rúðólfr. On the early missionary bishops, their impact, background and historical representation see, e.g., Melsteð 1912–14, 823–28; Einar Arnórsson 1930, 75–81; Jón Stefánsson 1950; Magnús Már Lárusson 1959a; Jón Jóhannesson 1956–58, I 167–73; Sveinbjörn Rafnsson 1977; Hjalti Hugason 2000, 126–40, 143–51; Orri Vésteinsson 2000, 20–21. The fundamental interpretive framework of Norse Christianisation and its missionary aspects is primarily established in Ljungberg 1938; Paasche 1958 [1941]; Birkeli 1973; see also Birkeli 1982. For the cultural and religious context of missionary activity and the spread of Christian learning see further Skre 1998; Sanmark 2004; Steinunn Kristjánsdóttir 2007. The oldest known contemporary reference to a foreign cleric in Iceland, presumably spreading Christian learning through missionary activities, is in the eleventh-century German poem *Merigarto*, whose author claims to have met this priest, Reginpreht, in Utrecht (see Maurer 1855–56, I 599; Orri Vésteinsson 2000, 20).

[7] See further Köhne 1972; 1974; 1987. On Ísleifr's presumed fasts in Herford see *Skarðsárbók* . . . 1958–66, 189.

[8] See further Björn Karel Þórólfsson 1956, 7–8; Magnús Már Lárusson 1967 [1956], 53; Hjalti Hugason 2000, 263–65.

[9] See also Einar Arnórsson 1930, 104; Björn Karel Þórólfsson 1956, 8; Bjarni Sigurðsson 1986, 43; Orri Vésteinsson 2000, 188; Hjalti Hugason 2000, 265–70.

Introduction xi

in the acquisition of a local saint at Hólar in 1200, when the locals settled on the first bishop, Jón Ǫgmundarson, as their first saint (he narrowly beat Brandr's predecessor Bjǫrn who also seems to have been a strong candidate for sanctity) (*Jóns saga ins helga*, 255–56, 298; *Guðmundar saga* A, 106–07; cf. Magnús Már Lárusson 1962, 610).

Bishop Ísleifr is reported to have taught young men who went on to illustrious Church careers.[10] Presumably books were used in his teaching and by his son Teitr Ísleifsson, also a celebrated teacher of the late eleventh century.[11] Thus book production in late eleventh- and early twelfth-century Iceland was probably strongly linked to the introduction of education for priests, Latin learning and the emergence of important cultural centres with schools, such as Skálaholt.[12]

We do not know much about these books. The author of the mid-twelfth-century *Fyrsta málfræðiritgerðin* mentions four types of writing: law, genealogy, the works of Ari fróði and 'þýðingar helgar', now believed to be homilies and sermons (*The First Grammatical Treatise* 1972, 208; cf. Sverrir Tómasson 1992, 429–31). On the other hand, it is believed that the earliest translations of legends stem from the latter part of the twelfth century, preceding indigenous hagiographies such as the legend of St Þorlákr. Thus the legends of Mary and the apostles, as well as those of famous martyrs, ascetics and fathers of the Church, are likely to have existed in Icelandic before St Þorlákr was translated,[13] and to have served as models for the

---

[10] *Hungrvaka* (9), following *Íslendingabók* (20), specifically names Bishop Kolr in Víkin and St Jón (see also *Kristni saga*, 39).

[11] Among his students were Ari fróði and Bishops Þorlákr Runólfsson of Skálaholt and Bjǫrn Gilsson of Hólar. His son, Hallr *electus*, must also have studied under him (*Íslendingabók*, 20; *Jóns saga ins helga*, 182; Hjalti Hugason 2000, 232).

[12] See Paasche 1914, 58–63; Melsted 1903–30, III 114–26; Benjamín Kristjánsson 1947; 1958, 195–202; Halldór Hermannsson 1958, x; Jón Jóhannesson 1956–58, I 187–91; Magnús Már Lárusson 1963a; Jakob Benediktsson 1970; Walter 1971; Líndal 1974, 260–63; Foote 1975; Orri Vésteinsson 2000, 59–60, 144–45, 150, 182; Sverrir Tómasson 1988, 18–44; Hjalti Hugason 2000, 225–32; Gunnar F. Guðmundsson 2000, 171–74; Cormack 2005, 28–30.

[13] For the rise and cultural context of hagiographical legendary literature in Iceland see, e.g., Finnur Jónsson 1920–24, II 863–77; III 90–97; Mogk 1904, 331–45; Turville-Petre 1953, 109–42; Magerøy 1961; Foote 1962; Widding, Bekker-Nielsen and Shook 1963; Bekker-Nielsen 1965; Widding 1965; Widding and Bekker-Nielsen 1965; Collings 1969; Carlsson 1972; Jónas Kristjánsson 1975, 261–70; Jørgensen, 1982; Samuelson 1977; Cormack 1994; 2005; Sverrir Tómasson 1992; 1993; 2007; Wolf 1993a; 1993b; 2003; Kratz 1993; Kirby 1993. A recent collection on Scandinavian sanctity with helpful references is DuBois, ed., 2008. A short but

subsequent *vitae* of this first Icelandic saint, which were composed in both Latin and Icelandic, although only fragments of the Latin texts remain.[14]

3

When Þorlákr died, Icelanders were probably starting to feel the need for a local saint. This would have been a practical need, but no less religious for that. While also bringing money and prestige to Skálaholt and to Iceland as a whole, the emergence of a local cult would have given Icelanders a saint they could identify with more easily than, for example, Italian martyrs of another millennium. Some of this intimacy is clear in the miracle narratives of St Þorlákr. Like all saints, he is seen as an intermediary between the suffering man and God himself, sometimes appearing along with another saint, such as the fourth-century saints Blaise and Vitus, to assist an Icelander in need (*Þorláks saga*, 88 (A), 197 (B), 284–85 (C)).

Þorlákr was an ideal candidate to become the first Icelandic saint. In the absence of martyrs and ascetics, a bishop was perhaps the most likely pioneer,[15] and among the first nine bishops of Iceland (the others being Ísleifr, Gizurr, Jón, the first Þorlákr, Ketill, Magnús, Bjǫrn and Klœngr), he seems to have stood out, for his own personal virtues, such as celibacy, for his contribution to general morality in Iceland (his *Penitentials*, for example) and for his attempt to question, criticise and improve the morals of the Icelandic élite, rigorously following the letters of his superior, the archbishop of Niðaróss.[16]

---

authoritative survey of wider perspective, including references to critical entries, is Heffernan 2003, cf. his earlier standard Heffernan 1988.

[14] On the Latin texts see note 30 below.

[15] From the ninth century onwards saints were traditionally recruited from high church officials, episcopal as well as monastic (see Wolf 2008, 243).

[16] St Þorlákr must be seen in the papal and archiepiscopal context of reformist objectives, see Bull 1915; Bugge 1916; Holtzmann 1938; Joys 1948, 136–89; Johnsen, 1951a; 1967; Kolsrud 1958, 186–202; Helle 1974, 45–52, 57–68, 85–89; 1981; Bagge 1981; Orrman 2003, 443–55; Coviaux 2006. More specifically on St Þorlákr's programme and its local context see Magnús Stefánsson 1975, 94–98, 104–08; Guðrún Ása Grímsdóttir 1982; Orri Vésteinsson 2000, 167–78, esp. 167–72; Gunnar F. Guðmundsson 2000, 25–38, cf. also 42–47; Ásdís Egilsdóttir 2002, esp. xxxiv–xxxviii; Björn Þórðarson [1953]; Jón Viðar Sigurðsson 2006, 499–502. Relevant archiepiscopal and papal letters are edited in *DI*, I 218–23, 258–64, 284–91, 298–302, 355–69. On the *Penitentials* see Sveinbjörn Rafnsson 1982a; 1982b; 1985; Gunnar F. Guðmundsson 2000, 31–34; cf. *DI*, I 237–44.

Later narrative sources also emphasise Þorlákr's championship of the rights of the Church to control church property, which is refashioned into a kind of adventure tale in the late-thirteenth-century *Oddaverja þáttr* within the B-version of *Þorláks saga*, with Jón Loptsson as the main antagonist (*Þorláks saga*, 163–81). This issue does not seem quite so important in the early-thirteenth-century sources, such as the *Þorláks saga* in this volume, however, where this conflict is referred to only in passing and Jón Loptsson is not mentioned in this context (cf. note 28 below).

Þorlákr was in many ways exceptional as a church leader in Iceland. Soon after he was born at the farm Hlíðarendi in 1133, his parents were forced to separate for financial reasons. This calamity turned out to be his good fortune, as he was sent to Oddi to study with Eyjólfr Sæmundarson, son of the renowned scholar Sæmundr inn fróði ('the Learned'). Eyjólfr was the uncle of the magnate Jón Loptsson, and he was also related, more distantly, to Bishop Brandr Sæmundarson of Hólar.[17] Thus Þorlákr became the protégé of one of the most affluent and powerful families in Iceland, which also had strong ties with the Icelandic church and, along with the family of Ísleifr Gizurarson, dominated it until the middle of the thirteenth century.[18]

After his studies with Eyjólfr he was sent abroad to study at the cathedral school in Lincoln in England, and in France, possibly at the school of St Victor in Paris where many notable Scandinavian church leaders were educated in the middle of the twelfth century.[19] Þorlákr would have been exposed to the newly emerging ideas of the French church and he might also have met future leaders of the West Nordic church, such as the archbishops Eysteinn, Eiríkr and Þórir, who all studied at St Victor and whose reigns at Niðaróss lasted from 1161 to 1214.[20]

---

[17] Loðmundr Svartsson of Oddi was the great-grandfather of both Eyjólfr and Brandr through the direct male line (Ásdís Egilsdóttir 2002, clv, clvii).

[18] For reviews of early ecclesiastical and episcopal politics, especially among the Oddaverjar and Haukdælir families, see Ármann Jakobsson 2000; Orri Vésteinsson 2000, 144–78, esp. 144–60. On the power of the Oddaverjar in general see, e.g., Helgi Þorláksson 1989; Jón Thor Haraldsson 1988. On fosterage see Magnús Már Lárusson 1959b.

[19] Þorlákr's education is discussed in Gunnar F. Guðmundsson 2000, 27–30. On the Victorine school in Paris and its reformist context see, e.g., Sicard 1991; Ferrulo 1985, esp. 27–44. On Lincoln see Owen 1971.

[20] Eysteinn Erlendsson (r.1161–88), Eiríkr Ívarsson (r.1189–1205) and Þórir víkverski Guðmundsson (r.1206–14). Their ecclesiastical and intellectual connections with Paris are treated in Bekker-Nielsen 1968; 1976; Johnsen 1945; 1951b.

Once back in Iceland Þorlákr became an important church reformer as the founding father of Iceland's first Augustinian monastery, Þykkvabœr, in 1168.[21] He was therefore in a strong position to replace Bishop Klœngr when he fell ill in 1174. His main rivals were another reforming abbot from Flatey, and Páll Sǫlvason priest of Reykjaholt, who clearly held an important position in the small élite dominating the Icelandic church in the late twelfth century. Páll, though, was probably almost as old as Klœngr himself, and neither rival seems to have been as accomplished as the foreign-educated Þorlákr, who also had the advantages of personal virtue and the patronage of the Oddi family (*Hungrvaka*, 40).[22] According to the saga the main obstacle to Þorlákr's victory was his lack of fame in Iceland; the other contenders were apparently much better known to the clergy of the diocese, and Þorlákr's aversion to the Alþingi, with its petty strifes and mediated justice, mentioned in his saga, may have contributed to his obscurity.

According to the saga the decision was left to Bishop Klœngr who chose Þorlákr. It is hard to say why he cast his vote in this way. Klœngr was from the North himself and somewhat of an outsider in Skálaholt; no other bishop of Skálaholt before 1237 had a more tenuous connection with the Oddi-Haukadalr élite (see notes 18 and 22). He had also proved a somewhat troublesome bishop, owing to his extravagant spending and above all his ambitious building enterprise at Skálaholt.[23] The saga, in spite of its general caution, states succinctly that Skálaholt was more or less bankrupt when Þorlákr arrived there, and one of the main reasons for electing a successor during Klœngr's lifetime was that the finances of the See could not be left to this ageing and ailing spendthrift. The saga also makes clear that Þorlákr took the financial matters of the See firmly in hand, along with Jón Loptsson and Gizurr Hallsson, who seem at that stage to have been acting as the power behind the throne.

What happened later is less clear. According to *Oddaverja þáttr* conflict broke out between Þorlákr and Jón in the first years of Þorlákr's reign, and they certainly seem to have had some disagreement, although the B-version's account of the conflict seems exaggerated. Gizurr Hallsson, on

---

[21] Gunnar F. Guðmundsson 2000, 30; Orri Vésteinsson 2000, 133–43, esp. 136; Jón Jóhannesson 1956–58, I 227–36; Magnús Már Lárusson 1963b; Janus Jónsson 1887.

[22] See Ármann Jakobsson 2000, 176–78; Orri Vésteinsson 2000, 152–54.

[23] This greatly concerned the author of *Hungrvaka*: 'Alls staðar skín í gegn áhugi á fjármálum og hag staðar og kirkju' (Everywhere an interest in the finances and material wellbeing of the seat and the church shines through) (*Hungrvaka* 35–36, 40; see Ásdís Egilsdóttir 2002, xv).

the other hand, kept on good terms with Þorlákr, although the archbishop had admonished him, along with Jón Loptsson, for keeping a concubine ('having two wives', *DI*, I 262–64). As lawspeaker in the 1180s Gizurr was the country's only lay official, and, having assumed office late in life, seems to have retired from other duties and spent most of his term in Skálaholt (1186–1200). Presumably he was there to support Þorlákr, rather than to act as a backseat driver, although one suspects he may have done a bit of both.[24] There is no reason to doubt his admiration for Þorlákr, however, and his part in his elevation to sainthood was probably substantial. His speech at Þorlákr's funeral serves as a milestone on the bishop's way to sainthood, and he also seems to have been quite knowledgeable about the previous bishop of Skálaholt, so it seems not out of the question that he had a hand in a plan to write not only what eventually became the A-version of *Þorláks saga*, but also *Hungrvaka*, the story of Þorlákr's five predecessors, which mentions Gizurr Hallsson as the main source (*Hungrvaka*, 3). The two texts could very well be from the same hand, as their style is not dissimilar.[25]

While the younger versions of *Þorláks saga* emphasise Þorlákr's conflict with the magnates of Iceland and his sufferings in office, the A-version presents him first and foremost as an ideal figure who enjoyed far more respect than most bishops. Though the author does not shy away from his differences with notable men, his period in office is for the most part depicted as a time of glorious success. This seems convincing, to the extent that Þorlákr clearly enjoyed great respect and that his elevation to sainthood involved the joint effort of the whole élite in Iceland. On the other hand, it may be significant that this happened a year after the death of Jón Loptsson, as Jón not only had been his main antagonist but was also the father of his successor and related to most of the magnates who promoted Þorlákr's cult.

---

[24] *Páls saga byskups*, 300, 304, 308, 312; cf. Ármann Jakobsson 2000, 176–78.
[25] Ever since the nineteenth century common authorship of *Hungrvaka* and *Páls saga*, and sometimes *Þorláks saga* as well, has been suggested. Guðbrandur Vigfússon (1858, xxxi–xxxiv, supported by Hannes Þorsteinsson 1912) argued for common authorship of all, tentatively suggesting Ketill Hermundarson as the author; Finnur Jónsson (1920–24, 561, 567–68) split *Þorláks saga* from the other two; Einar Ól. Sveinsson (1954, 13) suggested Þórir the priest as author of *Hungrvaka* and *Páls saga*; Sveinbjörn Rafnsson's argument (1993, 9–44) for Bishop Páll's authorship of *Hungrvaka* and his son Loptr's of *Páls saga* has been met with scepticism by Ásdís Egilsdóttir (2002, cxxviii–cxxxii; for a general review of authorship xxi–xxiii, xxvii–xxix).

4

Three main versions of *Þorláks saga* exist in Icelandic, as well as a text in Latin and collections of miracles. The main manuscript of *Þorláks saga* A, the version translated here, is Stockh. Perg. fol. no. 5, from *c*.1360. There is also an older fragment of the A-version, AM 383 4to, from *c*.1250. The B-version is generally believed to have been composed 60–80 years later than the A-version (perhaps during the reign of Árni Þorláksson, bishop 1269–98), and is preserved in the early-fourteenth-century MS AM 382 4to, with some fragments in British Library MS Add. 11242. There is also a C-version with further miracles, which is much closer to B than A, preserved in seven manuscripts, some medieval.[26] Guðbrandur Vigfússon and Jón Sigurðsson published both A- and B-versions, using C to fill the lacunae in B.[27] Ásdís Egilsdóttir does the same in her edition, which has formed the basis of this translation (*Þorláks saga*). As this suggests, the C-version's textual significance is fairly slight save for its additional miracles.

The main difference between the A-version of the saga and the B/C-versions is that the latter include additional material, mostly dealing with Þorlákr's tribulations in office. Presumably these are added to emphasise the sufferings that must precede holiness. In a new prologue it is said that Þorlákr did not spare his own body from the sword of persecution, and the saga duly includes graphic depictions of his conflict with magnates, mainly Jón Loptsson, which are absent from the A-version.[28]

This conflict was the result of a disagreement over control of church property, an issue that arose again in the 1270s, and thus it is not surprising that a saga composed in that era should emphasise this earlier claim. On the other hand, the main emphasis is still not on control over church

---

[26] For a recent thorough overview of versions A, B and C and their manuscript traditions see Ásdís Egilsdóttir 2002, xxxi–lii; see also *Ordbog* 3, 412; Jón Helgason 1976, 388–90.

[27] *Þorláks biskups saga, hin elzta* and *Þorláks biskups saga, hin yngri*.

[28] For this and what follows on the differing representations in the A- and B-versions of conflicts over ecclesiastical authority, *staðamál*, and the consequent debates on the historicity in this respect of *Þorláks saga* (specifically *Oddaverja þáttr*), see Guðbrandur Vigfússon 1858, xliii–xliv; Finnur Jónsson 1920–24, II 571; Mogk 1904, 792; Jón Helgason 1950, 14; 1976; Jón Jóhannesson 1956–58, I 216–20; Skovgaard-Petersen 1960, esp. 258–60; Jón Böðvarsson 1968; Magnús Stefánsson 1975, 96–104; Jónas Kristjánsson 1975, 243–44; Sverrir Tómasson 1992, 475–78; Astås 1994; Ármann Jakobsson and Ásdís Egilsdóttir 1998; 1999; Orri Vésteinsson 2000, 112–32, esp. 116–19; Ásdís Egilsdóttir 2002, xxxii–lii, esp. xxxii–xliv.

property but on Jón Loptsson's immoral affair with the bishop's sister and the latter's attempt to force him to give up this concubine, as well as on the immorality of other chieftains with whom Þorlákr had to deal. These events are not omitted in the A-version but merely referred to, in accordance with this version's overall tendency to emphasise the general over the particular.

It seems likely that the B-version exaggerates Þorlákr's claims regarding church property, since no more nearly contemporary sources (such as earlier bishops' sagas or *Sturlunga saga*) indicate that this was a heated issue in the 1180s. The saga itself remarks that Þorlákr got nowhere with his claims, and one might wonder if he really did pursue them as ardently as the saga insists, or whether it suited his successor, Bishop Árni Þorláksson, to portray Þorlákr as just as driven and energetic in this matter as he was himself. On the other hand, both control over church property and the morality of chieftains were issues that the archbishop of Niðaróss was raising at the time, and there is no question that there was a conflict between Þorlákr and Jón Loptsson, even though the B-version's dramatic account of it may be exaggerated. Since scholars have noted some factual errors in *Oddaverja þáttr*, the A-version may be more reliable on this score.[29]

It is generally assumed that both the A- and the B-versions of *Þorláks saga* differ, each in its own way, from an original saga which may have existed in both Latin and Icelandic, or only in Latin. A few Latin fragments about Þorlákr exist, of which the oldest (in AM 386 4to) may be from *c*.1200. These include a text about Bishop Klœngr and his ascetic ways which has been omitted from both the extant A- and B-versions. Ásdís Egilsdóttir has compared these texts to the Icelandic versions and concluded that the Latin text was fuller in some respects, shorter in others (2002, cix–cxxiv).[30] We may thus regard it as yet another *Þorláks saga*.

---

[29] The historical and ecclesiastical context of *staðamál* is treated in Jón Jóhannesson 1956–58, II 89–109; Björn Þorsteinsson 1978, 129–43, 202–09; Guðrún Ása Grímsdóttir 1998, xxvii–xli; Gunnar F. Guðmundsson 2000, 34–36, 84–93; Magnús Stefánsson 1978, 123–30; 2000; 2002; 2005. More generally on proprietary churches as an ecclesiastical phenomenon see Magnús Már Lárusson 1968.

[30] There are four fragments: AM 386 4to I from *c*.1200 (Lat. I), AM 386 4to II from the early thirteenth century (Lat. II), AM 670e 4to 24–26 and 28–30 (Árni Magnússon's copy of a no longer extant medieval manuscript), a fragment in The National Archive of Iceland from the later fourteenth century (Lat. III) and a liturgical text in *Breviarium Nidrosiense* from 1519 (Lat. IV). See edited texts in *Byskupa sǫgur* 1938–78, 159–74; *Latínubrot um Þorlák byskup* (including a translation into Modern Icelandic by Gottskálk Jensson); cf. also *Brot af Þorláks sǫgu hini elztu* and *Latínsk lesbókarbrot um Þorlák*. Kirsten Wolf has translated

The miracles of Þorlákr are related in various texts. In addition to the miracles concisely related in the A-, B- and C-versions are those collected in *Jarteinabók elzta,* which dates from *c.*1200. There are also two later collections of miracles appended to two of the C manuscripts.[31] While these miracle collections share some material, they vary a great deal in style and content. The two C collections are the most extensive and tend to emphasise the particular, firmly tying each miracle to a place or a person, in some cases even a year (the latest date being 1325). *Jarteinabók elzta* seems on the other hand to be intended for a foreign audience, as names of individuals and places are glossed as if unfamiliar ('a noble magnate called Gizurr', 'a good farm named Breiðabólstaðr'), and they are usually not geographically located with any precision.[32]

5

It has already been mentioned that *Þorláks saga* A emphasises the general rather than the particular. This is particularly evident in the part of the saga dealing with Þorlákr's years in office. His actions are not listed year by year but presented in an account of his general behaviour. Very few names are mentioned and the saga tends to avoid particular cases when describing Þorlákr's customs. He is said to have admonished some priests who were less virtuous than they should have been, but none is identified. There is much talk of Þorlákr defending the institution of marriage but, unlike *Oddaverja þáttr* with its narrative of the affairs of Bæjar-Högni and Jón Loptsson, the saga names no names in that context either. The passage of time is absent from Þorlákr's reign; his behaviour remains constant throughout these fifteen years. It is clear that, to this author, the saint transcends time in remaining with his community after death.[33]

---

the Latin fragments into English (1989). See Bjarni Aðalbjarnarson 1958; Jakob Benediktsson 1969; Gottskálk Þór Jensson 2003; 2004; 2009.

[31] For edited texts see *Jarteinabók Þorláks byskups in forna, Jarteinabók Þorláks byskups önnur, Þorláks saga byskups C,* and the earlier (1858) standard editions *Jarteinabók Þorláks frá 1199, Önnur jarteinabók Þorláks, Jarteinir úr Þorláks sögu hinni ýngstu;* cf. also note 2 above.

[32] The miracle collections and their textual and cultural contexts are addressed in Einar Ól. Sveinsson 1936; Holtsmark 1938; Loth 1984; Seip 1963; Piebenga 1993; Kratz 1994; Kuhn 1994; Whaley 1994; Ásdís Egilsdóttir 2002, lxxx–cviii. For Scandinavian context see, e.g., Gad 1961; Lundén 1950. For the place of miracles in medieval mentality and culture see, e.g., Ward 1982; Finucane 1977.

[33] For comparison between the A-version's hagiographical generality and the transformed focus in the B-version on particularities, see especially Ásdís Egilsdóttir 2002, lii–lxxx; cf. also entries cited in note 28 above.

In the account of Þorlákr's early years the historico-biographical tradition is more prominent. The saga relates his birth, education and consecration, including a claim that he was urged to marry but decided against it with the help of advice in a dream from a noble-looking man, presumably some emissary of God, not to marry since the Church is to be his bride. He then enters the canonical order, first along with Bjarnheðinn at Kirkjubœr and then as the abbot of the monastery of Þykkvabœr. Þorlákr thus becomes the first bishop of Iceland who is also an Augustinian monk. The account is interspersed with biblical quotations, showing that the narrative of Þorlákr's life has a religious function and a clear moral. This is a life encompassed in the edicts of the Bible, with frequent references to the Pauline letters.[34]

The style of the saga resembles the learned style of Old Icelandic translations of religious texts from the twelfth century which tends to be simple and straightforward.[35] It is slightly less sparse and succinct than the prose style of the Sagas of Icelanders, which may have developed this characteristic in the late thirteenth and early fourteenth centuries. The sentences are often longer, sometimes confusingly so. The author is not shy of making judgements and interpreting the life of the saint, putting it into the proper context of a *vita*.

The last part of the saga deals with Þorlákr's death and his subsequent cult and miracles. This is a narrative replete with people, even though most of them are not mentioned by name. The main emphasis in this part is St Þorlákr's function in his community. He is in the background now, as the supernatural helper invoked by the distinguished as well as the poor, the young and the despairing. He helps people find their fishing hooks and fetters, sets seals and whales adrift on the shores where people who need the meat can find them, and can even send two ships in opposite directions, each aided by a favourable wind. He cures hands, throats, eyes and gastric diseases, rids people of kidney-stones and helps the blind to see again. He helps those who get burned and those who are possessed by demons. A local saint, like a country doctor, cannot specialise too much. Þorlákr comes to the lowly and the great, and gives aid in minor as well as major trouble.

The author ends by emphasising Þorlákr's fame. He is a saint not only for Iceland but for all the North. He is venerated in Norway, England, Sweden, Denmark, Greenland, Shetland, Orkney and Caithness. Thus, according to his saga, Þorlákr is more famous than Iceland itself. In a

---

[34] See the notes to the text for relevant biblical quotations. The indispensable reference source is Kirby 1976–80.

[35] On this style, see e.g. Þorleifur Hauksson and Þórir Óskarsson 1994, 183–96.

country desperate for attention from the outside world, as Iceland has tended to be, this makes him a true culture hero.

6

One might expect *Þorláks saga,* as a religious text, to have been read aloud frequently in Skálaholt and presumably in other centres of the Icelandic church, to a mixed but devoted audience.[36] The text has a function within the cult of the saint and the author is palpably aware of this. The narrative is replete with moral learning, clearly aimed at the faithful for their moral and spiritual advancement. Þorlákr's life becomes a vehicle for the wisdom of St Paul, the Gospels and the Psalms. His studies with Eyjólfr bring to the author's mind the importance of the *imitatio Christi*. Þorlákr and Bjarnheðinn together remind him of the apostles going two and two together into the world, becoming 'the light of the world'. Þorlákr's lack of renown before his election as bishop becomes a lesson in humility. And Þorlákr's lack of eloquence and his sufferings when speaking in public demonstrate that it is not always by eloquence that a man can lead, he can also teach by his own good example (*docere verbo et exemplo*).[37]

Þorlákr is clearly established in the narrative as a role model for clerics and all virtuous men. One of the things that can be gained from his good example is a love for books and reading and his audience might well have been thankful that he also loved stories, songs, music and dreams. Indeed Þorlákr sometimes comes across as devout to the point of dullness, but the only thing he seems to have disapproved of is *leikar* 'games' which are unfortunately not depicted in detail: perhaps the word refers to major sporting events or to those types of game where money is wagered and changes hands.

In spite of an emphasis on St Þorlákr's strictness and some allusions to his stern rebukes, he is portrayed as a loving and a much-loved saint. It is

---

[36] On the recitation of hagiographical legends see Sverrir Tómasson 1988, 303–23 (with extensive citations of primary and secondary literature illuminating recitations in general); see also Sverrir Tómasson 1982, 11; 1992, 422–23. On *les* and *ræðingar* (*lectiones*), *lesbækr* (*lectionaria*) and *bréfer* (*breviaria*) see Helander 1957; Gjerløw 1965.

[37] This is acknowledged by Gregory the Great in his *Cura pastoralis* and increasingly adopted as a maxim in the twelfth century, primarily by Augustinian canons. See Bynum 1979; 1982. Although Gregory's *Dialogi* was probably more widely read than the *Pastoral Care,* the latter was well-known in Skálaholt: the first bishop Þorlákr had it recited on his deathbed (*Hungrvaka*, 26). Gregory's presence in early Icelandic learning is made evident in Boyer 1973.

less clear who loved him. Unlike St Jón of Hólar, who is shown within a thriving community of clerics, students, scholars and hermits, Þorlákr is alone on the stage of his tale.[38] Hardly anyone else is mentioned by name; the emphasis is on Þorlákr alone, a virtuous man singular in his saintly behaviour and his close relationship with God.

7

Þorláks saga was first published in 1858 in the edition of Jón Sigurðsson and Guðbrandur Vigfússon, which included the A- and B-versions (*Biskupa sögur* 1858–78). Guðni Jónsson used this edition in his popular edition of the *Biskupa sögur* (*Byskupa sögur* 1948, reprinted 1981), which contained *Þorláks saga* A, *Oddaverja þáttr* and some additional miracle collections. Jón Helgason in 1950 produced a facsimile edition of Stockh. Perg. No. 5, which includes *Þorláks saga* (the A-version), *Jóns saga* and *Guðmundar saga* (*Byskupa sögur* ... 1950) and in 1978 edited *Þorláks saga*, concentrating on the A-version but including additional material from the B- and C-versions, as well as the additional miracle collections and the Latin fragments (*Byskupa sǫgur* 1938–78). His edition had no introduction but proved very useful to later editors. Ásdís Egilsdóttir was responsible for a popular edition of the A-version of the saga in 1989 in connection with the visit of the Pope to Iceland (*Þorláks saga helga* ... 1989), and in 2002 edited *Þorláks saga* for the *Íslenzk fornrit* series. This is now the definitive edition of *Þorláks saga*, including the A- and B/C-versions, all the medieval miracle collections and the Latin fragments of the saga. It has an extensive and informative introduction and detailed notes, and has formed the basis for the present translation.

Despite these several editions of the Icelandic text, this is the first translation of the saga into English to be published since 1895 (Leith 1895). The syntax of the original is sometimes tortuous and the expression often oblique. This translation aims to make the sense as clear as possible whilst retaining the flavour of the author's style. While David Clark has mainly been responsible for the translation and Ármann Jakobsson for the introduction and notes, the two have collaborated closely throughout the project.

---

[38] A recent and thorough analysis of the style, characteristics and general outlook of *Jóns saga helga* is found in Foote 2003.

THE SAGA OF BISHOP ÞORLÁKR

CHAPTER ONE

At the time when Pope Anacletus ruled God's Church,[1] and Magnús Sigurðarson and Haraldr Gilchrist were kings over Norway,[2] Saint Þorlákr was born in the region in Iceland which is called Fljótshlíð, at the farmstead called Hlíðarendi,[3] in the year Bishop Þorlákr Runólfsson died.[4] They bore the same name not because he was named after Bishop Þorlákr, but rather because that One who knows all and rules all wanted to honour the earlier Bishop Þorlákr, so that his name would always be loved and exalted by all those people who have been destined since to hear and to know the glory of the blessed Bishop Þorlákr. Almighty God has granted that glory to the blessed bishop's name of which Solomon the Wise spoke formerly, saying that a good name was better than great riches.[5] And truly it was a good name, sanctified in holy baptism and blessed afterwards with episcopal rank. In this the proverb has proved true that 'what the wise say comes to pass',[6] since that name is now better than much gold to the many who call upon him in their need. It has proved no less true in this case, in so far as Holy Scripture says in another place that 'a good name is better than costly ointment',[7] since it now often turns out that a cure is speedily brought about by the invocation of his name for what could not be healed before, either by ointments or by those medicines which people had used and tried in vain.

CHAPTER TWO

Þorlákr's father was Þórhallr and his mother Halla. They were popular and accomplished: he had been a merchant before he established his household, and she was thrifty and very wise.[8] They were both of good family and had distinguished ancestors.[9] And it can now be seen clearly that God has eminently fulfilled what he promised us by the mouth of David the prophet: that the kindred of the righteous would be blessed,[10] and it can be seen that this has now been fulfilled beautifully and come to pass in the life of the blessed Bishop Þorlákr. Þorlákr's closest kinsmen were righteous and upstanding; the family was large but its funds insufficient.

Þorlákr was young when his father and mother broke up their household.[11] He was unlike most young people in his upbringing, easily guided and compliant in everything. He was obedient and endeared himself to all, was quiet and reserved in everything, able and eager to learn from an early age. He had studied the psalter before the separation of his mother and father's children, but he had scant other book-learning at first. However, from an early age he was already so attentive that many wise men spoke admiringly of him.[12] And, although he did not have much formal learning in childhood, he behaved as though he had learned nearly everything that might become him better than before. He had nothing to do with games or loose living. He was alert and even-tempered, and it could soon be seen that he would follow that counsel which David teaches in the psalter: that a man must turn away from evil and do good, seek peace and pursue it.[13]

CHAPTER THREE

When his mother saw in her wisdom, with divine foresight,[14] what an excellent cleric Þorlákr might become from his good mode of life if his education continued, then mother and son entered the most important centre of Oddi[15] under the protection of Eyjólfr Sæmundarson the priest,[16] who had both great authority and sound learning, and a greater share of virtue and good sense than most others. And we have heard the blessed Þorlákr bear witness about him, that it seemed to him he had scarcely ever encountered such an excellent man as he was,[17] and he showed afterwards concerning his master that he did not want to let pass away from him the wholesome counsel which the blessed Apostle Paul gave to his disciples, addressing his listeners thus: 'Be imitators of me as I am of Christ',[18] for it often happened when we praised his upright behaviour[19] that he said it followed the customs of Eyjólfr Sæmundarson his foster-father.[20] It was fitting that he praised him highly in his conversation, because he was indebted to him.

Eyjólfr valued Þorlákr most of all of his disciples in everything which pertained to the priesthood, for he saw from his wisdom and his conduct what afterwards proved true, that he would rise above them all in this, as is told later.

Þorlákr took holy orders at an early age when he was made a deacon by Bishop Magnús, and he was fifteen years old when the bishop died. And his ordination proceeded quickly because the authorities found that he himself paid attention to and heeded to the utmost the obligations which pertained to each of the ordinations that he received.[21] And as quickly as his education and ordination proceeded, he foresightedly attained with resolute steadfastness all the good qualities which belonged to the orders. He bore in mind, while his learning was smaller and his orders lesser, what the wise and holy Bishop Isidore says: that it is useful both to learn much and to live rightly, but if both cannot be achieved then it is more glorious to live well.[22] He also took care, though humility and service accompanied the lesser ordinations rather than the great honour of worldly esteem, that he held to all those virtues which ought to accompany the lesser offices, when he was elevated to the higher duties and esteem with the greater orders. This was his employment from an early age: that he spent a long time at his reading and was often writing, in between he was at prayer, and, when nothing else hindered him, he learned what his mother could teach him: genealogy and family history.[23]

CHAPTER FOUR

After Bishop Magnús had died there was for a time no bishop at Skálaholt, and few clerics were being ordained. It was then decided to ask Bishop Bjǫrn to perform ordinations at the Althing,[24] and he acceded to the people's request and Þorlákr was ordained as priest then along with many other clerics.[25] And when he was priest and he himself took up the rule and the oversight of services, it quickly became clear how careful and attentive he would be about his services and in all else that was placed in his charge with the ordination he had received. He then still proceeded humbly in his actions as before and accepted for himself in the first years of his priesthood small but profitable parishes and kept them for a time,[26] and it turned out well for him in terms both of money and of popularity, for pretty much everyone who was near him loved him dearly. Many good precedents have also been set by the blessed Þorlákr which have been scarce with many others,[27] in that he was at the same time both young and old: young in age but old in counsel. He then clothed himself anew in many virtues and most of all that virtue which David called the most needful for clerics: that they should clothe themselves with helpful counsel and righteousness;[28] and he showed it afterwards all his life in that he almost never let slip out of his hands what needed to be done, and all who were in his neighbourhood benefited.

And when things had proceeded in this way for some time and he had become well off, he became eager to journey abroad, for he wanted to explore the way of life of other good men. So he travelled from Iceland, but nothing is told of his travels until he came to Paris and he remained at school there as long as he deemed necessary for the study of what he wanted to learn there. From there he went to England and was at Lincoln and undertook much further study there, profitable both to himself and to others,[29] and he then had a lot of good things to share in his teachings since he was scarcely so well instructed before as he was now.

And when he had been away from Iceland for six years he went back to visit his kinsmen and native land, and his family and foster-brothers and all his loving friends rejoiced,[30] and his mother and his sisters above all, since they had the greatest interest in it but the greatest loss if anything had hindered his coming back. His mother accompanied him continuously after he came back to Iceland, and he lovingly granted aid to his sisters: Ragnheiðr, mother of Páll (who afterwards became bishop after Bishop Þorlákr), and the other, Eyvǫr, and for a very long time he was greatly vexed by their behaviour, which was not to his way of thinking.[31] And yet it came to a good conclusion at last, with God's grace and the good management of those people who had a part in it and their own goodwill. He still exhibited the same humility, or more, when he came back from his journey as he had had before, and he had not sought showiness or the finery of this world, as does many another who gains less furtherance and good fortune in their going away than he had gained. It is also the custom of many men that they equip themselves more carefully with weapons and clothes when they come back from a voyage, when they have more choice concerning such things than has been given to them before. But as the fruits of his journey, Þorlákr displayed learning and humility and many good customs which he had seen on his journey in many good men, bishops and other learned and upright men, those who have come closer to the place where God's Church originated and has since grown stronger.

CHAPTER FIVE

Þorlákr remained with his kinsmen for some years and he then had a very sizeable amount of property in his hands. And many wise men who were near him saw that he was then even better-disposed with regard to many things that were great and good—which were very important—than before he went away.

And no long time had passed before Þorlákr's kinsmen urged that he should establish himself somewhat better than was then the case, and they wished most of all that he would marry. It seemed to them that they could see that he was a man of means and a prudent man in most things. But God's Church has long grown strong and increased in might, and the obligations of learned men have also grown in terms of ordinances, because then not much fault was found by the authorities even if priests married widows, but now that is forbidden.[32] But then those women in the district who seemed to be the best matches were widows. Now Þorlákr was urged to adopt this course of action, and he then went along with his kinsmen to the farmstead called Háfr and intended to ask for the hand of that worthy widow who lived there, and they were received very well indeed there.[33]

But when they went to sleep after receiving fine hospitality, the very same night a man of noble appearance and in seemly clothing appeared to Þorlákr in a dream, and he spoke: 'What would your mission be here,' he says, 'if you could decide?'

Þorlákr answered: 'I do not know what will happen,' he says.

The one who appeared to him in the dream spoke: 'I know,' he said, 'that you intend to ask for a wife here. But you must not let that matter come up, because that will not happen. A much better bride is intended for you, and you shall take no other.'

And when he had spoken this, he vanished from his sight and Þorlákr wakes up. And he was then so dissuaded from this matter that he never asked for a woman's hand from that time on. They went away and Þorlákr and the woman were good friends ever after. But his companions found it rather strange that he was so changeable in this matter until they knew what had occurred, but then all who knew about it were content. After this whole incident his mind was not kindled to pride, though it had been revealed to him by God that he intended a better destiny for him than his kinsmen had intended and he himself had consented to. He rather embraced humility all the more firmly, following the example of all the best people, who have all become the more humble the higher they have gone up in God's sight—following the wise counsel of Almighty God when he says that everyone who humbles himself will be raised up,[34] and 'learn from me, for I am gentle and humble in my heart, and you will find rest for your souls.'[35] And before things had long gone on in this way, it quickly became clear what he had in mind.

CHAPTER SIX

At that time an excellent cleric led the farmstead called Kirkjubœr at Síða. He was called Bjarnheðinn and in the judgement of the whole people was the most excellent of men.[36] He was a wise and popular man, generous and eloquent, gentle and very learned.[37] And when each of them learned about the other—he and Þorlákr—then each of them became eager to live together with the other, and God granted that to them since he is accustomed to grant righteous men their just desires. And Þorlákr then went to stay at Kirkjubœr[38] and remained there for six years in total, and they then experienced that which God says: that 'my yoke is easy and my burden is light.'[39] That was both because strong beasts of burden were placed under the yoke and also because they bore it easily, for they then started to bear nearly all the responsibilities on behalf of all those people inhabiting the districts close by them. They also dealt with their subordinates in such a way that they took from them the heavy burdens which had been laid on them because of their offences and abusive language against God and good men, and because of their indulgence of the devil, and laid upon them instead God's light and mild burdens, in easily borne penances and undemanding acts of atonement. They took upon themselves in a remarkable way those names by which Almighty God called his apostles the light of the world,[40] because they lit up the path of mercy which leads to eternal rejoicing both with their excellent teaching in words and with their glorious examples.[41] It could be seen in their daily behaviour that they seldom forgot what God said to his disciples: 'Let your light shine before men,' he said, 'so that they may perceive your good deeds. Glorify your father who is in heaven.'[42]

Those who were with them felt as if there were nearly no times in which they might not have something good from them. They were also so like-minded and in agreement about good, as Luke says about God's apostles, that it might seem as if they had a single heart and a single soul.[43] It then spread widely around the district how unlike most men they seemed to be in their way of life. It then at once became the talk of wise men that there was nowhere more promising to look than there, to find that man best fitted to carry the heaviest burden in Iceland—and that was not a misjudgement, as it later turned out.

CHAPTER SEVEN

A man called Þorkell managed the second-best farmstead in the district; he was wealthy in possessions and wise in understanding.[44] And when he started to get on a little and had no close relations to inherit after him, then he endowed his kinsmen with money,[45] but retained at his own disposal the large and fine property that was left. He then made it known that he wished to choose Christ and His holy men as the heirs of all the property that was left, and wanted to found a canonical order in Þykkvabœr. But that matter was difficult to arrange at first, and because of this he sought first to get what was most difficult—the man who might establish the rule, which those men who wanted to settle upon a chaste life there should follow. He went then to Kirkjubœr and urged Þorlákr to undertake it, and he was not very difficult to persuade because he had already had it in mind to forsake the world and place himself under rule,[46] according to the words of Almighty God, when he declares no one able to be his disciple fully unless he leaves all his possessions for God's sake and then serves him afterwards with a pure heart.[47] And yet he enquired of Priest Bjarnheðinn how that would suit him or how advisable it seemed to him that he accept the responsibility that had been asked of him. And Bjarnheðinn said that it would seem to him a momentous day when Þorlákr decided to move away from Kirkjubœr. And yet he declared he was not greatly disposed to discourage him from what he saw that the salvation of many men depended upon.

Then a canonical house was established at Þykkvabœr with the advice and guidance of Bishop Klœngr and of all the people of the district, and then Þorlákr moved there, and a canonical order was then established there.[48] And the day that Þorlákr went away for good from Kirkjubœr all the people followed him out of the farmstead and they took parting from him very much to heart. And when Bjarnheðinn came home he looked into Þorlákr's bed-space and spoke very earnestly, saying that that particular place would never again be equally well occupied if Þorlákr did not occupy it himself. Þorlákr also said all his life afterwards, which was to the credit both of the place and of those who managed it, that he had never been so content with his lot as in those six years when he was at Kirkjubœr, and this place has in many ways been highly honoured, and not least because it may very likely seem that the place where he was happiest will have been the best.

Þorlákr was fully thirty-five years old when he moved to Ver and he stayed there for seven years. He first took ordination as a canon and was at first appointed prior over the canons who were there, and he at once ordered their life so beautifully that it was remarked by wise men that they had never seen such good conduct where there had been a regular life for so short a time as there. And later Bishop Klœngr consecrated Þorlákr as abbot of Ver, and he then began anew to hold a remarkable rule over the brothers over whom he was set.[49] He commanded them to maintain love and concord between them and explained to them how much was at stake, since the Son of God says that wherever two or three gathered together in his name that he would be among them.[50] He upheld the strictest conduct on their behalf, and indeed they behaved well in every regard.

CHAPTER EIGHT

Halla, Þorlákr's mother, was with him his whole life while she lived, but he had settled money on both his sisters before he resolved upon the monastic life. He was affectionately disposed toward all his kinsmen then as before, and a spiritual father to all of those over whom he was placed. He forbade the brothers any roaming about and all journeys for which there was no necessity,[51] but bade them be steadfast in all good things in their service, just as the Apostle Paul has taught in his epistle: 'Pray without ceasing', he says, 'and give thanks to God in all things.'[52] God's Son Himself also says that everyone will be saved if he stands firm in good deeds right up until the end of his life.[53] He bade them carefully maintain silence when that was due, but use wholesome language when conversation was permitted, and according to the words of the Apostle Paul: 'Evil speech,' he says, 'destroys good conduct.'[54] It can also be seen why one ought in this life to keep oneself from worldly and evil words, if it is even wrong for good to be spoken when one should be silent, as David says in the Psalms: 'I am humble,' he said, 'and I kept silent over good things.'[55] He seemed humble because he was always more eager to speak good than evil, and yet he often refrained from both of them for God's sake.

Men went to Abbot Þorlákr's canon's seat from other monasteries or places of the Rule, both his own countrymen and foreigners, to see and to learn good conduct there, and each one who went there bore witness that they had never been to a place in which the life seemed to have been lived as beautifully as the one Þorlákr had established. Then, for the first time, many men realised that there was much good to be seen where he was on account of his goodness, which others had not managed to bring about themselves. Many of those who came to meet him with various troubles went away whole after meeting him when he gave them his blessing and chanted over them.

Many other things happened to him which many regarded even then as miracles. This event occurred while he was staying there that the house caught fire, but when Þorlákr came and blessed the house the fire abated. If the livestock sickened then they always recovered with his chanting over them, if they were destined to live.[56] His consecration of water was remarkable, for both men and cattle were cured by it. If water that Þorlákr had consecrated was sprinkled over the cattle then they were almost never harmed by sickness, weather or wild beasts. If mice did harm to food or clothes then their numbers were reduced or they disappeared altogether because of the water which was sprinkled over them, and if the people did everything as he advised. The water then soon travelled around all the neighbouring region and around the whole of Iceland after Þorlákr became bishop, because people everywhere seemed to find in it a remedy for that for which there was most need. And yet wise men were wary, in speaking, of calling them plain miracles or of attributing them to his extraordinary holiness, because so speaks Holy Scripture: 'You shall not praise a man in his lifetime. Praise him after his life and magnify him according to the merit of his life.'[57] And it is so spoken for this reason: that it may become a responsibility, both to those who speak before the end of someone's life is fully known, and it may also be that this thought itself entices the mind of the man toward pride. And it can now be seen how well this has turned out, that men have followed wholesome counsel in this matter, since few praised him overmuch in life but now they seek to praise and glorify him in every way they can, now that they know his glory and holiness.

CHAPTER NINE

As the conduct and life of Saint Þorlákr shone with such a blossom of purity and goodness and fair prudence in all other matters as has just been said,[58] Almighty God caused the way to be prepared for what he had previously planned: that his honour should be magnified and grow from what it was then. And it happened in this way, that when Bishop Klœngr became overcome with age,[59] he was stricken with a serious illness. His legs broke out in sores, and he then became completely incapable of performing his office on account of illness. However, he had received permission from Archbishop Eysteinn for a man to be selected as bishop after him.[60] Bishop Klœngr went to the Althing then and asked of his friends that a man should be chosen to journey abroad,[61] and meetings were set up for it.

That same summer, as if sent by God, Abbot Þorlákr went to the Althing because it seemed to him necessary to go, since it was never his custom to go from home unnecessarily. When the discussion began about this matter three men were nominated for election who seemed best suited in every way, and one of them was Abbot Þorlákr. The second abbot was called Ǫgmundr, a very notable man; the third man was a priest who was called Páll, a great scholar and a successful farmer.[62] It bore fine witness to each of them that each felt most eager to support the one that he knew best. But it worked against Þorlákr that he had not much exalted himself in that pride which is called conceit,[63] and he praised his good deeds more in the sight of God than of men, and he strove more to surpass other men in goodness rather than to appear so in the eyes of those of little discernment. And the result was that he seemed to many the least well-known of those who were up for election, and this was understandable because he had not been a very close neighbour to many men in their homes and regions.

Þorlákr was reticent at this meeting, but many of the others, who accrued less credit from their big words than he, had much to say. It was then enquired of Þorkell Geirason, whose truthfulness was known and who of wise and noble men was most knowledgeable about Þorlákr's conduct, what kind of leader Þorlákr might be or how eloquent he might be. But Þorkell answered: 'Þorlákr strives,' he says, 'to *do* everything best rather than to talk most.'

People were pleased with this answer, and many at once regarded Þorlákr with more affection when they heard such worthy testimony to his mode of life from such a wise and even-tempered man. The conclusion of the matter was that the election was devolved to Bishop Klœngr, so that he was to choose from those who were under consideration. And he chose Þorlákr to journey abroad and to take consecration as bishop after him and all the responsibility which belonged to it.[64]

Lord Abbot Þorlákr went from the Thing back to his canonry, and asked Bishop Klœngr to have the management of the see and church that season.[65] And then the finances of Skálaholt became very difficult: there were large expenses but small donations. He was not able to travel on his visits, and all the gifts ceased and things could not go on like this every season as if there were no need for substantial provisions.

CHAPTER TEN

After Christmas men were sent from Skálaholt for the bishop-elect, and he travelled from the east at Lent and Jón Loptsson, who was then the greatest chieftain in Iceland, along with him, and they came to the church in Skálaholt half a month before Easter, and Gizurr Hallsson was there already.[66] There were also other men there, who were the bishop's friends and the pillars of the community. Þorlákr then took up the oversight of the church, and a large debt was incurred then at once for those necessities which the estate had to have.[67] He then immediately had great trouble, both because of the unwanted presence of men[68] and other difficulties about which he was troubled, but he bore them all patiently.

Bishop Klœngr lay in bed with little strength and Þorlákr remained at Skálaholt, because men did not want him to travel abroad on account of the hostilities which then existed between Norway and Iceland,[69] since there were unsettled cases which had arisen between the lands from killings and property seizures, and that delayed him for some years. But when Bishop Klœngr died[70] and the time came that it seemed to him necessary that Skálaholt should not be without a bishop any longer than had already been the case, he did not allow himself to be held back any longer from the journey abroad. It made no difference that he was dissuaded from going on account of the hostilities. He adopted the words of the Apostle Paul: 'You should not tremble in fear of wicked men,' he said.[71] Then he was ready to go abroad, and he wished to have neither much money, compared to what others had had, nor any great entourage, and he got on well with his journey until they reached Norway.

CHAPTER ELEVEN

When Bishop-Elect Þorlákr[72] came to meet Archbishop Eysteinn,[73] he received him remarkably well and quickly let it be known that he would happily do everything on his part that he deemed his duty, but he would not give him the rank of bishop unless the king's consent had been obtained. Ruling over Norway then were the father and son—King Magnús and Jarl Erlingr, his father[74]—and they took Þorlákr's whole case badly and from them came threats instead of relief such that neither property nor men would be safe. But Þorlákr paid that little heed and thereby showed his steadfastness to be just as David teaches in the Psalter, that 'it is better to trust God than chieftains',[75] and because of this he let it pass. But the archbishop felt he was in great difficulties because he wanted to love both parties, and he wished to heed what the Apostle Paul teaches in his epistle: 'Fear God,' he says, 'and honour the king'.[76] It could also be seen in everything that he wanted to honour both parties fully in this matter. The archbishop then bore messages between them and other well-intentioned men, and it came about that the king and the jarl consented to Þorlákr taking consecration as bishop, and the appearance of friendship was brought about between them and they gave each other gifts before they parted. And King Sverrir, who was both noteworthy in speech and wise in understanding, often mentioned that everything went easiest for the father and son when there was friendship between them all and Þorlákr remained in the land, both in battle and nearly everything else.[77]

Then Þorlákr was consecrated as bishop by Archbishop Eysteinn in the days of Pope Alexander,[78] three nights after the passion-day of the Apostle Peter.[79] Present at the consecration was Bishop Eiríkr of Stafangr who later was Archbishop in Þrándheimr after Archbishop Eysteinn.[80] The third present at Bishop Þorlákr's consecration was Páll, bishop of Bergen, a most outstanding man and a friend of Bishop Þorlákr all his life afterwards.[81]

Bishop Þorlákr remained only a short time with the archbishop after he had been consecrated because he knew full well how urgent the need was for his return to Iceland and the sheep over whom he had been set. And when Bishop Þorlákr had parted from the archbishop, the other bishops asked what he had thought of Bishop Þorlákr.

He said that he thought he had never consecrated a bishop[82] whom he deemed fully his equal in all the qualities which a bishop should have, as the Apostle Paul says in the epistle which he sent to Titus: 'It is fitting,' he said, 'that a bishop be innocent and educated, diffident and no drinker, open-handed, not avaricious, clever and kind-hearted, helpful and hospitable, upright and honest, spotless in life and sage in counsel, true and trustworthy, kind and quick of speech, affectionate with folk but harsh with the heedless.'[83] And one can see it is for a holy man to follow that way of life.

'I cannot tell you how wise his way of life has seemed to me,' said the archbishop, 'better than by saying that I would choose to have the last day of my life such as I saw every one of his days to be.' And it can now be seen how wise and clear-sighted he was about the state of the blessed Bishop Þorlákr.

CHAPTER TWELVE

When summer came Þorlákr took passage in a ship and put out to sea with his companions and had a good voyage, and they took harbour where they would have chosen, and the bishop came home to Skálaholt the day before the Feast of St Laurence.[84] People were very glad at his coming and he began at once calmly to rule in those matters which came before him with authoritative probity. He nevertheless closely maintained the canonical rule in everything that he could bring about when he was made bishop: in terms of dress and of vigils and fasts and prayer-meetings. He began to reform the household customs and home affairs, which reforms were well kept in his day in many respects.

Bishop Þorlákr felt most love and affection for those priests and clerics who lived chastely and held their offices in approximately the way appointed, and honourably regarded and happily established them as far as it was in his power to do so. But those clerics who set less store by good behaviour and held their offices unwarily he admonished with kindly commands to do better and turn their conduct into the right path along with the conduct of those for whom they had to answer. But those who were not moved by soft admonitions he rebuked with stern words in moderation and gentle chastisement, just as the Apostle Paul taught Timothy: 'You shall warn and pray and rebuke with all patience and the aim of instruction.'[85]

He thought carefully about the church's property and always set men over its financial administration so that he himself might be as free as possible from that occupation, and still the assets of the church were augmented as far as was possible, and still they had everything that they needed. [86] And his management of financial matters was so judicious that all wise men soon spoke of how good his guidance seemed to be in all matters.[87]

And, however much time he spent in the disposition of that which pertained to the property so that it all proceeded in the best manner, he nonetheless gave the most thought to what pertained to the church and that the clerics were provided for as well as possible in every way. Moreover, it went along with this that he also took great pains over all the divine services of the clerics and lovingly taught them all the services which their ordination obliged them to perform. He gathered together clerics for the highest festivals in Skálaholt and explained what each of them should do so that all that they were obliged to perform proceeded beautifully in the sight of God. And as much as he took pains over others, he himself did everything best so that nearly everyone could distinguish him from most other clerics in terms of how excellently he performed all services in God's sight so that it was a delight to see and hear.

Bishop Þorlákr often taught lessons, and that was a great trial because speech was difficult and painful for him, but the words were so sweet and well put together that what David says in the psalter always came into the minds of those who listened to his lessons: that 'sweeter are your utterances in my throat, O Lord,' he says, 'than honey and the honeycomb in my mouth.'[88] Bishop Þorlákr bore out the same utterances of God by setting such a beautiful example by his life that none so glorious could be found in the life of any person living at the same time.

Bishop Þorlákr kept long vigils at night when others slept, and prayed earnestly that he might achieve for himself what God promised: 'Blessed is that servant,' he says, 'whom the Lord finds keeping watch when he comes to visit him.'[89] And that is also mentioned in God's commandment when he speaks thus himself: 'Watch,' he says, 'for you do not know at what time the Lord will come.'[90] And it has proved that these hours were seldom out of Þorlákr's mind, because now has come about for him what God promised to those who were often found in wise vigils: that he would place them over all good things belonging to him after this life.[91]

CHAPTER THIRTEEN

Bishop Þorlákr the Holy fasted often when he was home at his see and in this he bore in mind what the Lord himself said in the Gospel, that there were some kinds of demonic temptations which cannot be overcome except with fasting and praying,[92] and he therefore let the same be seen in his life: that he wanted to rise above all demonic temptations. He consoled those who had been sorrowful and told them what the Lord himself said: that blessed are those who mourn now for they shall afterwards be comforted,[93] and what Christ said to his apostles in another Gospel: 'Your sorrow shall be turned into rejoicing,' he says.[94]

Bishop Þorlákr reconciled and brought into agreement those who had been wrathful and discordant and told them, as was said and is true, that anger greatly blunts men's integrity while it continues, as the Apostle Paul says, that God's righteousness and the wrath of man have nothing in common,[95] and in another place: 'Do not be overcome by evil, rather overcome evil with good,'[96] that is: to overcome anger with patience and goodness.

Bishop Þorlákr often looked on holy books and read over the holy scriptures, for he never forgot what the Apostle John says in his book: 'Blessed is the one who reads and hears the words of this book and guards those things which are written in it.'[97] He often taught clerics both to read books and other knowledge which was useful for them. He saw how much need there was to teach good things, as David says in the psalter: 'Come, my sons, and listen to me, and I will teach you how God is to be feared.'[98]

He was always writing, and always wrote holy books after the example of the Apostle Paul when he said in his epistle: 'We do not write to you anything other than what there is most need for you to read and to know.'[99] But whatever else Bishop Þorlákr did his lips were never still in God's praise and in prayer, for he was mindful of what the Apostle James says in his epistle: that the continual prayer of a righteous man can do much before God.[100] His prayer has indeed greatly helped both himself and many others.

The bishop was mild and gentle in all good counsels, and gave wholesome counsel concerning everything about which he was approached. He has now gained what God has promised to those who are of the disposition about which he speaks in the Gospel: 'Blessed are the meek, for they will gain the earth eternally.'[101]

CHAPTER FOURTEEN

Bishop Þorlákr sang Mass every day, both for his own salvation and that of others, and always bore in mind the Passion of God's Son, and he has now received a reward for his service all the more beautiful in proportion to how he celebrated that sacrament more often and in a more remarkable way than most other men. He took great pains to love poor people: he clothed the cold and fed the hungry, and it was obvious that it seldom left his thoughts what will occur at the Day of Judgement: how much rides on what was done in this life for the poor.[102] He also took pains, beyond what most good men before him have done, to have poor men called together for the highest festivals, twelve or nine or seven at a time,[103] and came secretly to wash their feet and then dried them with his hair and gave each of them generous alms before they went away.[104] And he acted so after God's example rather than men's: God who previously washed his disciples' feet and later allowed himself to be tortured to save all mankind. God's Son also spoke thus when he had washed his apostles' feet: 'Do according to my example that which I now do for you.'[105] The blessed Þorlákr therefore made the foot-washing precede the merciful gift. His intimate friends and confidants could not keep silent after his death about what they felt they knew clearly: that he had concealed within himself the acts of mortification and of charity which he believed no-one knew about, as God commands that the left hand shall not know what the right hand does.[106] And the bishop's intimate friends dared not reveal more openly afterwards what he himself wanted to have concealed thus.

Bishop Þorlákr was often accustomed to have discussions with good and pure men, and thus acquaint himself with their customs and strengthen them in their wholesome counsel so that they might maintain their virtue. He also placed careful guard on the conditions of those men who did <not> heed their misdeeds,[107] to lead them from wrongful desires and call them back to the correction of their affairs even though before they had not paid due heed,[108] because the Lord said: 'I do not desire the death of the sinful man,' he said, 'rather I desire that he turn to me and live.'[109] The blessed Bishop Þorlákr showed this to all of those who wished to repent of their faults, and if they wanted to follow his advice he was glad over them and gently helped them with light penances, according to what God's prophet said: that every day that a man wished to turn to God he would then live the good life and not die an evil death.[110] But those who would not be converted by his friendly admonition and not give up their misconduct at his rebuke, he put some under an indict and excommunicated some, according to what Christ commanded his disciples: 'You shall chastise your brothers lovingly, but if they will not be chastised then you shall loathe them as heretics or heathens.'[111] He patiently bore men's offences against him but greatly lamented men's misconduct and never agreed with the immorality of evil men because he was eager to obey what God says: 'Blessed are the long-suffering for they will be called the sons of God.'[112] Disobedient men pained him because he healed the spiritual wounds of his subordinates, just as was granted to the Apostle Paul concerning God's Church in his day so that no man had an injury or grief that it did not seem to him that he felt all their troubles because of his love for them.[113]

CHAPTER FIFTEEN

Holy Bishop Þorlákr used the authority which he was given at his consecration to bind and loose the unions of men on God's behalf,[114] so that the balance between both parties seemed to wise and righteous men to be observed, and neither fury or intemperance ever ensued. And indeed, difficult though it might be, he was never so faint-hearted or soft in this, that it could not be attributed more to meekness and mercy, even if he waited long for many, since a correct judgement was reached in the end.[115] He often let what David says come into his mind: that the Lord loves forgiveness and righteousness, and grants glory and mercy.[116]

It is also to be mentioned that Bishop Þorlákr most loved that place (secondly only to Skálaholt) which he had previously adorned with his presence. He consecrated as abbot in Ver Guðmundr Bjálfason, a good and righteous man, gentle and free of ambition.[117] Þorkell Geirason, who was mentioned earlier in this account,[118] placed himself under the Rule there and maintained it well while he lived; he died in the ninth year of Bishop Þorlákr's episcopate.

In the days of Bishop Þorlákr it was made law to keep holy St Ambrose's Day, St Cecilia's Day and St Agnes' Day, and to practise night fasts before the Feasts of the Apostles and St Nicholas' Mass.[119] He sternly commanded people to keep the Friday fast so that no one should eat twice on an ordinary Friday, except for the one in Easter week.[120] He kept Friday so strictly himself that he ate only fish and vegetable foods if he was in good health, but he was mild and moderate in this when he was ill, so that he ate white food on Ember Days and Fridays if he was asked to do so,[121] and set an example for those men who now wish to do the things that, it is to be hoped, will seem most fitting in the sight of God. Bishop Þorlákr was ill during his episcopate in the year when Christmas fell on a Friday, and he was weak and yet he ate meat that day and showed by his example that it was better done so.[122]

He took great pains to keep together those people who were joined in holy matrimony, but he laid a heavy share of fines and penances upon those people who seriously violated it. It seemed to him that it would be the greatest offence to God if the greatest enjoyment of this world which he has granted to men—and, for the sake of his love and mercies and the desires of men, made righteous and blessed what would otherwise be a cardinal sin—if that were wretchedly insulted and wrongly violated. But he never let the money which men paid for their misdeeds be added to other money; instead he contributed it for the purpose that those married couples who lived well together and were penniless might stay together as before, and that would serve those who had donated the money as some protection and penance for their wicked deeds.[123]

Bishop Þorlákr broke up all those unions which he knew to be unlawfully contracted in his days, whether greater or lesser men were involved. He was not wholly in agreement with some men, even chieftains,[124] because he agreed only with what was fitting. It seemed to him that it was an even greater downfall of God's Church if noble men erred greatly. He also deemed it no more excusable that they, who had previously had great credit from God both in wealth and in honour, should not restrain themselves from unlawful things.

CHAPTER SIXTEEN

Now it is to be told about the daily habits of the blessed Bishop Þorlákr: how even-tempered he was about good things. He never said a word that was not to some purpose if he was called upon for it. He was so careful in his speech that he never cursed the weather, as many do, nor any of those things which were not reprehensible and which he saw were according to God's will. He longed for no day to come.[125] He felt no great apprehension about anything except the Althing and Ember Days.[126] The Althing because it seemed to him many men who were highly thought of went astray in their suits there, and much seemed to him to lie at stake; but the Ember Days because it seemed to him a great and momentous responsibility to ordain men who had come a long way for it when he saw in them a serious incapacity, both on account of having little learning and of other behaviour which was disagreeable to him. However, he could hardly bear to deny them, both on account of their own poverty and for the sake of those men who had taught them or had sent their tokens for them.[127] But he told each of them clearly what obligations pertained to each ordination and caused the responsibility to fall on their own heads and those who sent them.

Þorlákr often allowed teaching to take place, for he saw that, although it was often not listened to as sensibly as written narratives should be,[128] nevertheless it hindered many men from unprofitable acts. He was so even-tempered in his fasts when he was at home, and in vigils and prayer whether he was at home or not, that the like could not be expected of anyone else. He consumed so little food that nothing else seemed more likely than that he would part from them when he suffered the most. As far as alcohol was concerned it was never apparent that it affected him, if he had this kind of drink. But he was so lucky with alcohol that ale never failed which he had blessed and made the sign of the cross over with his hands when it was being made. He was so unpretentious and friendly at those feasts where there was drinking that he suffered everything that was not unseemly. But when Bishop Þorlákr drank water or non-intoxicating liquor he proceeded with it so moderately and with such abstinence that he sipped three sips, or five, or seven, but almost never more.[129] He also almost never drank between meal-times unless he was sick, if it was not a public banquet.

Bishop Þorlákr was never completely well during his episcopate, and that was as was to be expected since the Apostle Paul says that strength is made perfect in sickness.[130] He often allowed healers to operate on him for his pain, and showed that God has established healers so that they should sometimes be able by God's will to stop long discomforts with brief pains.

Bishop Þorlákr had a more rational manner in his prayers than most other men. He first sang the *Credo* and *Pater Noster*,[131] after he had signed himself with the sign of the Cross, and the hymn *Jesu nostra redemptio*,[132] and he allowed it to be known at once that he thought continually upon the ransom with which God had redeemed mankind, and true love for God and men, the desire of everlasting bliss and life with God, the fear of Judgement Day and the Second Coming of the Creator to judge all mankind; all of which this hymn proclaims. Then he sang the Prayers of Gregory[133] while he got dressed and after that the first psalm from the psalter, and never let go out of his thoughts the wholesome counsel which stands in the psalm: that 'blessed is the one who does not go after evil counsel and does not consent to evil deeds with sinners and does not judge unjust judgements and always heeds God's laws'.[134] But when he came to church he first sang praise of the holy Trinity. After that he praised with song the holy men to whom the church was consecrated, which he was then in and where holy relics were kept. Afterwards he read the Hours of Mary,[135] and after that he laid himself down before the altar completely prostrate, where it was not hallowed, and prayed for a long time for all God's Church. And every day he sang a third of the psalter above and beyond his usual singing, whether he was at home or not, and sang more from amongst the psalms than other men.[136] He first sang the *Gloria Patri* for the holy Trinity,[137] then next the *Miserere mei Deus*,[138] then *Salvum fac Pater et Domine* for all Christian people.[139] But if a difficult case came before him he sang the verse with which Solomon the Wise prayed to God in his days: *Mitte mihi Domine auxilium de sancto*.[140] And when he went from the table he sang *Benedicam Dominum in omni tempore*,[141] and when he got undressed for sleep he sang the psalm where the Lord is reminded of his promise that they shall be safe who guard their ways justly and who offend others neither in words nor in deeds. This psalm is *Domine, quis habitabit*,[142] and it was his great delight to maintain such practices, and he hoped that some might imitate his custom. He took pleasure in stories and songs and in all stringed and other musical instruments, in wise men's speech and dreams and in all that in which good men's pleasure lay, except for games, because it seemed to him that this could hinder the profitless business of bad men.[143]

CHAPTER SEVENTEEN

Bishop Þorlákr dreamed a dream at the Althing where it seemed to him he went from the church there at the Thing back to his booth and he bore the head of the holy Martin in his embrace.[144] But Páll, the priest at Reykjaholt, a holy man,[145] interpreted the dream thus: that he himself would thereafter bear a holy bishop's head wherever he went. And it is now obvious to all that that is true. When the blessed Þorlákr had sat at the see at Skálaholt for fifteen years with honour and bright blossoms of all kinds of good deeds, beloved of God and of good men, merciful and upright, humble, patient and just, wearied by men's offences and by manifold illnesses besides, then he sought with his friends to give up the bishopric and submit himself afterwards to the same canonical rule. But Almighty God did not allow this to be brought about, for he saw his chastity and his virtuous life well sufficed for sanctity, though the honour which he had given him did not diminish at all in men's eyes.[146]

CHAPTER EIGHTEEN

The blessed Bishop Þorlákr travelled around the quarter nearest to him for the last time and on that journey acquired the illness which led him to the grave. He came back to Skálaholt with very little strength and lay in bed for three months and had a serious illness, but never such severe pain that he could not give counsel about everything and order things as he wished.

Gizurr Hallsson was then at Skálaholt, a great chieftain, wise and benevolent.[147] He often strengthened the blessed Þorlákr with beautiful parables about holy men who bore their pains valiantly for the sake of God. Páll, his sister's son, also came to find him in his illness, because the bishop loved him most out of his kinsmen, and many of the bishop's friends and loved ones came to him to receive wholesome counsel from him and to show him their love. Þorvaldr Gizurarson, a great chieftain, came there and the blessed Þorlákr reckoned up the see's financial affairs before the clerics and chieftains, and they had greatly strengthened while he had authority over it; and therefore, with their advice, he allotted some money to his poor kinsmen. He gave his best household items to the bishop who was to come after him and other things to priests, but the least valuable ones to poor people, because he never ignored them when he gave gifts to his friends. He gave a gold ring to Bishop Brandr,[148] but his consecration ring to Páll, his sister's son, and that was a prediction of his honour since he became bishop after him,[149] and all thought it was good to be allotted something that he had owned.

Seven nights before his passing he called clerics to him and had extreme unction administered to him, and before he was anointed he gave a long speech, though speaking was difficult for him: 'I lay in sickness once before, anointed and with little strength,' he said, 'and I decreed that all men who had been excommunicated by me should be free if I died. I intended that as a comfort to them but not as an admission of error on my part, but they credited that to me as if I thought I had gone too far against them when because of their crimes I excommunicated those who would not be admonished legally, and I commanded them to be released because I thought I was dying. But now I decree to you that all my pronouncements shall stand againt them unless they have reconciled themselves with the penances that I had previously ordained, or else they shall await the verdict of the bishop who comes after me.'

Then he rested and said again to those who were beside him: 'I want to ask you to forgive me if I have done anything to you of which you did not think well.'

But all said that they had nothing to be angry with him for. And Gizurr Hallsson spoke thus on behalf of all of them: 'We ask you, master, that you forgive us for the things we have done amiss toward you, which must be many and weighty.'

The blessed Þorlákr agreed to this forgiveness willingly. Then Gizurr uttered that speech which it is obvious the holy spirit spoke through him: 'We ask you, master, although you are now parting from us visibly in bodily presence, be to us a spiritual father, interceding for mercy with Almighty God, for we firmly believe that in the spiritual life you will have no less power with God than now.'

But Bishop Þorlákr answered nothing, in imitation of God's Son, when he agreed with something silently without saying a word, and he now grants to all what he was asked for then. But for the sake of humility he did not want to reveal that he was able to do this. And few who were by him then could forbear weeping for sorrow.

As the bishop saw that he said: 'Do not grieve though our living together is interrupted, for I go according to my destiny. I have always been capable of little if others have not helped me. I am little loss to you since next after me will come a great leader. I will comfort you in this, that I think I know certainly that God will not adjudge me a man doomed to hell.'

Afterwards he kissed the clerics and gave them blessings before he was anointed. But after the extreme unction he would not speak except for what there was most need for, but his lips always stirred in prayer while he was living.

And when seven nights had passed after the extreme unction, he asked for a change of clothes early on this day, but Ormr the priest, his chaplain,[150] answered thus: 'It seems to us, master, a great responsibility to move you; do you not want to be changed into these clothes if you have not long to live?'

The bishop answered: 'It will be fitting to move me, but I hope for mercy from God from the anointing and not from these clothes.'

Other clothes were then given to him and he maintained all that day the same good customs. And when evensong was finished a certain faintness came over him, and when he raised up his eyes he said: 'Where has Þorkell gone now?' But Gizurr Hallsson, that very wise man, considered that Þorkell had shown himself to the bishop at his death because he had most openly encouraged him from the worldly to the pure life.

But when Bishop Þorlákr had come to the point of death, he asked for something to drink. And when it was carried to him, he sank onto the pillows and fell asleep blessedly unto God, and God granted him that glory that he thirsted for at his death, just like God's Son Himself, nor could it be assuaged earlier than in the spiritual life, for which God's friends are always thirsty. In the death of the blessed Bishop Þorlákr God elucidated what he said earlier from the mouth of David: that the death of holy men would be glorious, because it seemed to all to be better to be beside him in death than by many living men.[151] It also occurred after his death that his face was much brighter than other men's, and his pupil was as bright in his eye as a living man's who was very sharp-sighted. Many wounds had befallen his body, great and small, but all were healed as soon as he had died, and all felt that this was a great matter but Gizurr the more because he could see more clearly than the others. Then the body was prepared and his hair cut. People now have that relic far and wide and derive much comfort from it.

Bishop Þorlákr died on Thursday, one night before Christmas Eve, at sixty years old, and he had been bishop for fifteen years. There had then passed 1186 years since the birth of Christ.[152]

CHAPTER NINETEEN

After the bishop's death his body was carried into the church and was kept in the choir for three nights to await burial. But he was laid in the earth on the second day of Christmas, and standing by were Priest Páll, his kinsman who became bishop after him, and many other learned men.

There came there also the body of a poor man who was leprous, and the bishop had taken him from poverty and looked after him until the day of his death, and God wanted his act of mercy to be shown, which was just one of many others.

But before men left the grave of the blessed Bishop Þorlákr, Gizurr Hallsson spoke about the events which had occurred, as was the custom at the burial of distinguished men. He told first of what a useful man Bishop Þorlákr had been both to the see and to all the people of the land. Then he spoke some words to the honour of those bishops who had had residence at the see of Skálaholt before Þorlákr had come.[153] After that he spoke thus:

'It is good to remember the witness and traditions of our ancestors about those bishops who lived before our memory, since the one whom they know best seems best to everyone, and as glorious men as they have all been in their episcopates, nevertheless it surpasses all how Þorlákr prepared himself for the dignity of bishop far beyond all others. He was chaste all his life, well-mannered and virtuous, liberal and just, merciful and wise of counsel, humble but strict, meek of temper with true love and affection for both God and men. He took consecration as a child and the wisest men decided to increase his honour and consecration while possible, and at a young age he placed himself under the holy Rule and maintained it right until death. Now although it is commanded that we should not let judgement be pronounced about the condition of a man, there must be few with a prospect of salvation if he is not full of bliss, as dissimilar as he was to most men in his life and good customs.'

He closed his speech with eloquent words.

The lay proprietors of the see and the people everywhere in the land grieved greatly over the death of the blessed Bishop Þorlákr, for they thought him to be more separated from people than has now proved to be the case, since never had the sanctity or miracles of any man emerged in Iceland before Bishop Þorlákr's, and yet many men were comforted by beautiful dreams where God illuminated his merit further. And yet then a very bad time and famine set in, with only one bishop in the land and he was very old,[154] and then unrest raised itself in the north.

It happened in Vatnsdalr that a truthful farmer dreamed that he seemed to have come outside and saw a man come from the south over the heath, and he asked him how Bishop Þorlákr was, and he answered: 'He is not called Þorlákr now, but rather Ruler with God.' The farmer told the dream to Abbot Karl and he interpreted it as meaning that the bishop would be dead and have glory with God.[155]

Gizurr Hallsson dreamed a little after the death of Bishop Þorlákr that he seemed to see him sitting on the church at Skálaholt in his bishop's robes and he was blessing the people from there. And he interpreted his dream as meaning that he would still be an overseer over his Church. Many wise men said that either the sanctity of Bishop Þorlákr must result, or otherwise this would not be destined for Iceland, of which Archbishop Eiríkr bore witness in the letter which he sent to Bishop Páll, saying thus: 'Our excellent brother, Bishop Þorlákr, of fine memory, we believe has been holy in his life, but is now a glorious gemstone of power before God and of great authority.'

CHAPTER TWENTY

A priest in the north who was called Þorvaldr[156] dreamed four years[157] after the death of Bishop Þorlákr that he came to him and told him when the weather would improve, for the winter was oppressive then: 'I give you this advice,' he said, 'that men seek my grave in the summer and see that my body is taken out of the earth, and if there seem to anyone to be signs of holiness there then men shall do as pleases them concerning my invocation and the keeping of my day.' He then disappeared. The priest told the dream to Bishop Brandr and offered to swear to it.

21.[158] During the winter, the eve of Maundy Thursday after the death of Bishop Þorlákr, a farmer called Sveinn saw such a great light in Skálaholt over Bishop Þorlákr's tomb that he could hardly see the church for it.

22. Priest Ormr went on a mission to the Althing during the following summer, on behalf of Bishop Brand, to recount what signs had occurred of Bishop Þorlákr's sanctity in those districts. And his horse exerted itself so hard in spots of snow[159] that it could not continue, but as soon as he invoked Bishop Þorlákr his horse jumped up and he rode a full day's journey to the Thing. And when this event had been told, and many others, then men were glad at this account and many men at once invoked Bishop Þorlákr in their need and it seemed to be well, but that was still without getting permission from the bishops.

23. Later the same summer Bishop Brandr sent Priest Ormr with his other clerics to the Althing and had his letter carried before Bishop Páll and the other chieftains, and there was then a testimony to the many miracles of Bishop Þorlákr. Then men had a meeting about this matter, and Bishop Páll was easy to lead and hesitant in these matters as with many others concerning the other chieftains of the land and the management of this joyous news.[160] Men's counsel along with Bishop Brandr's

message was that Bishop Páll declare in the place of legislature[161] on St Peter's Mass-day that all men should be allowed to invoke the blessed Bishop Þorlákr.[162] Men should sing services to him on his death day. At St Peter's Mass Bishop Þorlákr was chosen as bishop and then invocation of him was allowed, and the keeping of his mass-day was made law the second summer after this event. And, as a sign that God did not think this presumptuous, at once remarkable miracles occurred at the same Thing.

24. There was a man called Tjǫrvi; he suffered a great injury to his hands.[163] The hands went stiff and leprous so that he could not straighten his fingers, and that injury lasted for fifteen years. He invoked the blessed Bishop Þorlákr for his healing. He fell asleep after that and, when he wakened and wished to wash himself, his hands had been completely healed and they were shown to everyone who was present, and then the *Te Deum* was sung.[164] And as soon as this miracle had become known to all then one after another started to invoke the holy Bishop Þorlákr, and it was not strange, since the miraculous power was so great that it was granted almost before it was asked.

25. This event occurred at the same Thing, that Abbot Jón from Ver went down with serious bronchitis and swelled terribly so that he could eat nothing and could hardly speak so that it could be heard.[165] Then he invoked the blessed Bishop Þorlákr for his health and fell asleep immediately afterwards and awoke completely healed. This event was told to Bishop Páll.

26. The man called Guðmundr gríss, Bishop Páll's kinsman, had a serious throat disease, and he was both unable to eat and weak and he seemed to many men likely to die.[166] Then he called on his friend Bishop Þorlákr to intercede for him with God for such healing as he might see would best suit him. But when he had made this firm vow he improved from day to day and was completely well as soon as the taper had burned out in Skálaholt upon which he had made his vow, and he himself recounted this miracle to Bishop Páll and many other men.

27. The man from the Austfirðir called Sighvatr, of high lineage, suffered pain in the eyes so severe that he thought his eyes would burst if the pain did not lessen quickly.[167] He invoked the blessed Bishop Þorlákr. He became heavy with sleep immediately after the vow, and when he awakened all the pain had gone from his eyes, but the eyelids were red and swollen as a testimony to the pain which had been in his eyes.

28. There was a man called Unas.[168] He suffered an uncomfortable illness there at the Thing; he completely swelled up. His belly went up in front of

his breast and such a violent pain ensued that he could hardly stand. He later called with tears of compunction upon the holy Bishop Þorlákr for his healing. He became heavy with sleep immediately after that. He seemed to see the holy Bishop Þorlákr in a dream, and with him the blessed boy Vitus.[169] The bishop said to him: 'You will not benefit from your own behaviour if you become well, rather from the fact that God's time of mercy has now come in gifts of healing towards men.' He awoke completely healed.

29. A northern man also suffered a violent pain at the same Thing, an illness which at once bereft him of his wits. Then other men invoked the blessed Bishop Þorlákr for him and he at once became completely well.

30. A noble priest who was called Þórðr became dangerously ill at the dissolution of the Thing and men were afraid for him because he was a prominent man.[170] He then called on the blessed Bishop Þorlákr for his health to recover and his infirmity abated so quickly that he was able to leave the Thing with the other men, and he was in a short time completely well and praised God and the holy Bishop Þorlákr for his health.

31. At the Thing it occurred that a northern man lost his good sledge-straps, and they were searched for carefully and not found. And when their recovery seemed hopeless to him he called upon the blessed Bishop Þorlákr that the sledge-straps should be found, and at once they were found where they had most often been looked for, and they praised God and the holy Bishop Þorlákr.

32. There was a worthy man named Árni.[171] He had a great and dangerous pain inside his ribs. He called upon the holy Bishop Þorlákr to heal him and improved at once.

33. After the Thing it happened that Ormr, kinsman of the blessed Bishop Þorlákr and brother of Bishop Páll, was in the bath at Skálaholt and had it in his mind that he would love the sanctity of his kinsman more if he had a sign of it himself, and at that moment he scratched his right hand on his razor and it bled terribly and would not stop.[172] Then he called upon his kinsman and patron, Bishop Þorlákr, to stop the bleeding and never a drop came out after that.

34. There was a priest called Torfi, of noble extraction and well married, and his wife will be mentioned later in this narrative.[173] He suffered a severe pain in the eyes when he left the Thing and he could not sleep the night he was in Skálaholt. Then he called upon the holy Bishop Þorlákr and was then led to the church and there at his mass he received healing of his injury and went away completely well.

35. One good housewife also suffered great pain in the eyes and invoked Bishop Þorlákr and was healed at once.

36. Magnús Gizurarson, foster-son of the blessed Bishop Þorlákr, owned a good and productive farm.[174] But that difficulty occurred that the best part of the ewes ran away and could not be found, and it looked as if the greatest harm would happen: that the sheep would swell up and lose their milk. He then took the best course, as he frequently did, and called upon the holy Bishop Þorlákr, his foster-father. After that the sheep came from the heath, completely unswollen, towards those who sought them.

37. One young boy suffered severe pain in the eyes and bore it with difficulty, and the mother was very concerned. She then took the wick of a candle and laid it on the boy's head and invoked the holy Bishop Þorlákr and he was healed at once.

38. One poor man lost good fetters where there were extensive bogs thick with grass and it was unlikely that they would be found. He then called upon the holy Bishop Þorlákr that the straps should be found and they were found at once and the poor man was pleased.

39. One young man rode carelessly where there were volcanic vents and his horse's feet were burned so that people thought it would die. Then the blessed Bishop Þorlákr was invoked and in a few days the horse was healed completely. They gave thanks to God and to the holy Bishop Þorlákr for this incident.

40. One man suffered a large boil in his throat and became unable to speak. He directed his thoughts to invoke the holy Bishop Þorlákr. And the same night the boil burst and he was healed in a few nights.

41. There was one man who was so short-sighted that he could not see any better than to discern his own fingers, and he had been this way for a long time.[175] He called on the holy Þorlákr for his eyes and he at once became sharp-sighted.

42. The hand of one young man swelled up to such an extent that healers were not able to do anything. But as soon as the holy Þorlákr was called upon the hand was completely healed.

43. In a great overflowing of the rivers two chests were lost, one full of iron and artefacts and the other of clothes. The man who owned the chests called upon Bishop Þorlákr and the chests were found unspoiled with everything that was in them.[176]

44. In one town people came to an impassable river and those who called upon Bishop Þorlákr got over it safely, but those who did not call on him did not.

45. A young woman became so violent with terrible pains that men could hardly hold her. But as soon as Bishop Þorlákr was called upon for her then she at once was healed.

46. One woman had for many years had so much pain in her hand that she could not use it for anything. She called upon the holy Bishop Þorlákr for it and the next night afterwards she was whole.

47. Merchants in Iceland could in no way raise their anchor. But as soon as they called upon Bishop Þorlákr it came loose.

48. Many went by ship out from the Vestmannaeyjar and a rough sea and a storm came upon them so that they lay near death. They then called upon Bishop Þorlákr to help them and at once a great calm fell and the sea became tranquil and they reached harbour safely.

49. One housewife lost a good gold ring and it was searched for far and wide and frequently and not found. She called upon the holy Þorlákr and at once the ring was found where it had most often been sought.

50. One woman suffered such a violent sickness that her speech and wits left her. But as soon as the holy Bishop Þorlákr was invoked for her she became well.

51. One old priest broke his collar-bone and such pain and swelling set in that he became disabled. He called upon the holy Bishop Þorlákr for himself and he quickly became well.

52. A man sold a poor man a blind sheep and did not want to compensate him when he found out. The poor man called upon Bishop Þorlákr and the sheep regained its sight.

53. In one farmstead a thief stole a lot of goods. But those who suffered the loss called upon Bishop Þorlákr to compensate them for the loss, but it was a very poor season for food then. Then it struck them that they should go into the river with a net, and immediately they caught so many large salmon that their loss seemed to them well compensated.

54. The river called Holtavatn dammed up so that the sand was thrown up over it thirty fathoms deep.[177] That turned into a great loss for those men who owned meadows by the river. Then one farmer called upon the holy Bishop Þorlákr so that the digging out should go better than was usual. And the next day the river had broken out into the sea.

55. A ship drifted away from a man on account of a storm and inundation of water. But the man who lost the ship invoked Bishop Þorlákr and it had come back by the morning to the same landing place.

56. A young boy fell into the fire and burned his hand terribly. But his father and mother called upon Bishop Þorlákr for him and the hand was completely healed within three days.

57. A young boy fell into a tub of whey and seemed dead when he was pulled out. But the boy's father and mother called upon the holy Bishop Þorlákr for his life with great sorrow. And as soon as the vow was confirmed the ruddiness came back to his cheeks and after a long time dead he sprang up completely well.

58. One man swelled up terribly and the whole belly bloated and puffed up as big as an ox. But his wife invoked the holy Bishop Þorlákr for him and he quickly became healthy.[178]

59. When Bishop Páll had the miracles of Bishop Þorlákr read aloud at the Althing for the first time, a blind man and a deaf man who were standing by received their sight and hearing.

60. One woman fell into a hot spring at Reykjaholt and was terribly burned so that her flesh and skin stuck to her clothes. People called upon Bishop Þorlákr for her that her feet should not fall off, and she was completely well within a month.

61. One woman broke her leg and great pain and swelling ensued, and she lay for a long time in her bed and healers could not achieve any relief for her. She invoked the holy Bishop Þorlákr and that same night he came to her in her sleep and laid hands on the leg and she awakened completely well.

62. One man lost a great iron sledge-hammer in deep icefields. He called on Bishop Þorlákr and he found the sledge-hammer on land a day later.

63. Some merchants from Orkney were driven off course by a storm to the Faroes where there were cliffs and reefs, and it seemed certain death to all of them. They called on the holy Bishop Þorlákr and at once the storm turned into a favourable wind around them.

64. Other merchants had come to the point of death in the English Channel because of the storm and the height of the sea. They called upon Bishop Þorlákr and at once got a fair wind and balmy weather and thereafter a good harbour.

65. A man had epilepsy and pain in the eyes. He called upon the holy Bishop Þorlákr for his recovery and did not improve. He was tormented for a long time in this sickness, but one night he dreamed that Bishop Þorlákr came to him and said to him: 'I heard your cry to me, but you could not receive any healing because you have unconfessed crimes. Now confess yourself before a priest if you wish to receive healing.' Afterwards he woke up. And as soon as he had confessed, he became well.

66. A woman had a serious illness from a dreadful boil on her stomach for thirty years. She called upon the holy Bishop Þorlákr for her recovery. And during the night before the thirteenth day Bishop Þorlákr showed himself to her in a dream, and she awakened completely healed.

67. A young man was playing and his hand went out of joint and went back in with difficulty. Such pain and swelling ensued that he was incapacitated. He called upon Bishop Þorlákr, and in a dream he came to him and said: 'You are quick to make promises but not to fulfil them.' And when he awoke he remembered that he had made a vow to him and not fulfilled it. He discharged both his vows and then became completely whole.

68. A horse was maimed in being gelded so that its whole belly began to rot from the pus. The man who owned it vowed to give Bishop Þorlákr half the horse, and within half a month it was completely healed.

69. One man had a leg injury where the bone cavities were full of blood and pus, and the healers could not heal it at all. He called upon Bishop Þorlákr for his healing, and in a dream it seemed to him he came to him and stroked the leg, and he awoke completely healed.

70. One young boy sustained an acute illness where the abdomen broke open. The father and mother called upon Bishop Þorlákr for him and he at once became completely healed.

71. Again men called upon Bishop Þorlákr for a fair wind for themselves and they got a good wind. And when they sailed out along the fjord another ship sailed towards them with a strong wind, and they had called upon Bishop Þorlákr for a wind, and each of them by evening made the harbour they wanted.

72. Two women were travelling on a winter's day in a great frost and heavy weather into the icy part of the fjords. One of them went into labour far from any dwellings. They called upon Bishop Þorlákr to help them. Then men came to them and transported them to a farmstead. The child was gravely hurt from the frost so that its bones became crooked, and one of its eyes popped out onto its cheek and a wound

broke out on its body. The grief-stricken mother called upon the holy Bishop Þorlákr for some mercy for the child. Then she bound earth out of Þorlákr's tomb onto the child's eye and afterwards lay down and quickly fell asleep. It was then three o'clock in the afternoon, but by the middle of the evening the child awoke so completely healed that the eye had come back, blue in colour and sharp-sighted. All the wounds had healed up and all the child's twisted bones, but the eye which had been healed was a bad colour.[179]

73. At one farmstead in the Vestfirðir a house caught fire so that the whole farmstead seemed likely to burn, but there was no one at home except for young children. One child called upon Bishop Þorlákr for help and instantly there came such heavy rain from heaven that the fire went out, but the rain did not fall any more widely than on this farmstead.

74. A man fell from a cliff and his knee-cap and leg were damaged. He called upon Bishop Þorlákr and was quickly completely healed.

75. One poor housewife called upon Bishop Þorlákr to give her children something to eat because there was a great famine then. She went to the beach and saw a large seal. It lay there quietly as she went toward it as if it were stuck fast to the stone, and she killed it and that yielded enough provisions for her.

76. One hospitable farmer could not get a meal on account of the famine. He called upon Bishop Þorlákr for help and a little later a whale came to him as shore-drift where many men had ownership along with him. They made the whale fast and much disagreement arose amongst the men about the division. Then came such sharp weather that the fastenings broke and the whale which had drifted ashore broke out to sea and came afterwards to land which this farmer alone owned.

77. A poor farmer called upon Bishop Þorlákr for food in the famine. He went to the beach and laid down a fishing-line during the evening. And in the morning a whale as long as the fishing-line had been caught there.

78. A man rowed out to sea and pulled a large fish on board. The line broke and the fish swam out to sea with the hook. He called upon Bishop Þorlákr and a little later he found the fish drifted ashore with his hook and line in it.

79. A poor man's cow fell from a cliff and was completely smashed up. The poor man called upon Bishop Þorlákr and the cow was quickly completely healed.

80. A woman was possessed by the devil, but when men poured into her mouth oil which Bishop Þorlákr had consecrated, she became well at once.

81. A great tree fell upon a woman so that she was severely injured. But her husband invoked Bishop Þorlákr for her and she felt she saw him in a dream and awoke completely well.

CHAPTER EIGHTY-TWO

When so many unusual miracles of Bishop Þorlákr were revealed and read aloud, it was agreed among all the leading men in the land, clerical and lay, to take his body out of the earth. Therefore Bishop Páll called together clerics and chieftains to Skálaholt. First there was Bishop Brandr from Hólar, Priest Guðmundr Arason, who later was bishop,[180] Sæmundr and Ormr, brothers of Bishop Páll, Hallr and Þorvaldr and Magnús Gizurarson, Þorleifr from Hítardalr and many other chieftains.[181] There was great flooding of the rivers at that time throughout the whole land, but God wished that that impede no man from travelling to the see. And when they had all come together they all kept vigil during the night, to the praise of God and the holy Þorlákr.

During the following day his holy relics were taken out of the earth and carried into the church with hymns and songs of praise and beautiful processions and with all the honour and veneration which could be achieved in this land. The coffin was set down in the choir and clerics then sang the *Te Deum*, and sick men knelt at the coffin and many men were healed thereby.

A young man of high lineage who was called Þorsteinn, who had had a dangerous kidney-stone infection for a long time, was completely healed there so that the stone was flushed out of him, no smaller in size than a bean, and afterwards many signs occurred from the stone.[182]

There was a man called Uni who walked with a wooden leg because his leg was crippled, and he became completely healed there.[183]

A maiden crippled from childhood became completely well there, and God healed many other illnesses and pains through the merit of this excellent friend of his.

A young boy who had had epilepsy for a long time received healing there.

Then the coffin and Bishop Þorlákr's holy relics were carried into the place where he was venerated for a long time.

One poor man intended to go to Skálaholt on this day of glory because his fingers were completely pressed into his palms and the hands had totally withered, but he could not come and he met people who told many joyful tidings from Skálaholt. But he became sad that he had not been deserving of being there. He called then with tears upon the holy Þorlákr, and he became completely healed the next night afterwards.

In the same year that Bishop Þorlákr's holy relics were taken out of the earth many miracles occurred, which I will mention in a short narrative.

CHAPTER EIGHTY-THREE

Many sick people received healing, whatever kind of illnesses they languished in, if they called upon his name. If people were situated on sea or on land, whatever kind of peril they faced, they quickly received the remedy for their difficulties as soon as they called upon him, so that the winds subsided and the seas became calm, conflagrations were extinguished, floods abated, storms stilled, property that people lost was found, and if people bound earth out of his tomb on an injury, boil or sore, then it quickly improved. Cattle were restored from all kinds of sickness as soon as he was invoked.

Because of these benefits of the holy Bishop Þorlákr which I have now told, much money was given to the see at Skálaholt from all lands in which his name was known, most from Norway, a lot from England, Sweden, Denmark, Gautland, Gotland, Scotland, Orkney, the Faroes, Caithness, Shetland, Greenland, but most from within the country. And it can be observed what love people had for him from this: the first time that services were sung to him at the see, 130 wax candles were burned there.

Bishop Páll had a goldsmith named Þorsteinn make a shrine for the holy relics of Bishop Þorlákr which is there to this day, and that shrine now stands over the high altar at Skálaholt where God grants all kinds of miracles according to his merits.[184] The blind receive their sight there, the deaf their hearing, the crippled are made straight, the leprous are cleansed, the lame walk, the insane and demon-possessed receive full cures, captives are freed wherever in the lands they call upon his name.[185] The dumb receive the power of speech, and all kinds of internal illnesses and sicknesses improve there, and there is no injury of humans or cattle by sea or by land that God does not grant healing and help on account of the intercession of his blessed friend Bishop Þorlákr, as soon as he is invoked.

We pray now that he intercede for us with Almighty God for peace and prosperity and a good end to this life, and afterwards may he lead us to the heavenly lodging, freed from all the devil's power by his authority, that with him we may live blessedly with God in the court of heaven for ever and ever without end. Amen.

NOTES

[1] Anacletus II (b. 1090, d. 25 July 1138; consecrated 14 February 1130) was born Pietro Pierleoni. He was wealthy and from a powerful Roman family of recently converted Jews, studied in Paris and was a monk in Cluny under Abbot Pontius (abbot from 1109 until his deposition in 1122). Appointed cardinal deacon of Cosma and Damiano in 1106, and later a papal envoy, Anacletus II was elected as pope by the majority of the cardinals after the death of Honorius II. Important reformers such as Bernard of Clairvaux (1090–1153), however, supported Innocent II (d. 1143), who also gained the support of the Holy Roman Emperor. Anacletus II was thus declared antipope but was recognised in Scotland, Aquitaine, Milan and other Italian cities, and had control of Rome during his lifetime. He died before Innocent II, whose followers eventually gained the upper hand, and it is thus noteworthy that only Anacletus should be mentioned here. See Schmale 1961.

[2] Magnús and his uncle Haraldr were joint kings of Norway 1130–35. For their tumultuous reign see *Heimskringla* 1941–51, III 94–106.

[3] The first settler of Hlíðarendi was Baugr. His son was Gunnarr in Gunnarsholt, father of Hámundr, father of Gunnarr of Hlíðarendi, one of the main characters of *Njáls saga*. In the early thirteenth century it was occupied by Krákr, father of Hafliði and Jón of Egilsstaðir, who are mentioned in *Sturlunga saga*. Hafliði's daughter Þorgerðr married Magnús Agnarr Andrésson of the Oddi family. With her the farmstead seems to have passed to the Oddi family, who held it in the fourteenth century (*Landnámabók*, 348, 352–54; *Sturlunga saga*, I 363, 567).

[4] Þorlákr Runólfsson, third bishop of Skálaholt, was consecrated in 1118 and died in 1133. He is one of the five bishops whose stories are related in *Hungrvaka* (*Hungrvaka*, 22–28).

[5] Proverbs 22: 1. *Melius est nomen bonum quam divitiae multae* 'A good name is better than great riches'. Here and below the English translation used is that of the Douay-Rheims Bible.

[6] cf. 'Spá er spaks geta' (*Grettis saga* 1936, 104).

[7] Ecclesiastes 7: 2. *Melius est nomen bonum quam unguenta pretiosa* 'A good name is better than precious ointments'.

[8] The word *forvitra*, translated here as 'very wise', could also imply the gift of second sight.

[9] Þórhallr and Halla presumably separated before Þorlákr reached the age of ten, since Eyjólfr the priest is referred to as his foster-father (ch. 3). It seems reasonable to assume that Þorlákr spent at least five years with him before taking holy orders at fifteen. Halla is not mentioned when Þorlákr goes to Skálaholt (ch. 10), which might indicate that she died while Þorlákr was abbot (between 1170 and 1177). The families of Þorlákr and Halla are traced in *Byskupa ættir*. Þorlákr was descended directly in the paternal line from the settler Ketill einhendi. Among his other notable ancestors were Þorgils Örrabeinstjúpr, hero of *Flóamanna saga*, and Þóroddr, father of the well-known lawspeaker Skapti. Of the many other children of Þórhallr and Halla, only two daughters are named, Eyvǫr and Ragnheiðr (*Byskupa ættir*, 12).

[10] Psalms 111: 2. *Generatio rectorum benedicetur* 'the generation of the righteous shall be blessed'. Here and elsewhere the numbering of the Psalms is that of the Vulgate. In the imediately preceding passage the righteous are defined as those who fear and obey God (cf. Astås 1994).

[11] As is implied in the preceding paragraph, this separation seems to have been mostly due to poverty.

[12] These wise men are not named, in keeping with this author's custom of using names sparingly.

[13] Psalms 33: 15. *Diverte a malo et fac bonum, inquire pacem et persequaere eam* 'Turn away from evil and do good: seek after peace and pursue it'. Archbishop Þórir Guðmundsson of Niðaróss uses the same quotation to admonish the chieftains who had quarrelled with Bishop Guðmundr Arason (*Saga Guðmundar Arasonar Hólabiskups eptir Arngrím ábóta*, 90).

[14] The close relationship between mother and son may be a deliberate echo of that of St Augustine and his mother Monica. Þorlákr was an Augustinian monk and Monica was greatly venerated in the twelfth century (her translation occurred in 1162). See further Book 9 of St Augustine's *Confessiones*.

[15] This could mean that Jón Loptsson (who later lived at Oddi) and Þorlákr grew up together, but Jón is nine years older and may not have lived in Oddi, his uncle's residence, at the time.

[16] Eyjólfr was the son of Sæmundr fróði of Oddi, Jón Loptsson's uncle. He does not figure strongly in other narratives, but he and Hallr Teitsson are mentioned in *Hungrvaka* as the most important chieftains in the country after the death of Bishop Magnús Einarsson. Eyjólfr is believed to be older than his brother Loptr; he may have been born about 1090 but died in 1158, according to annals (*Hungrvaka*, 32; *Islandske Annaler indtil 1578* 1888, 116 (*Annales regii*); *Flateyjarbók* 1944–45, IV 302 (*Annáll*).

[17] The benevolent foster-father and instructor is a theme in the Icelandic bishops' sagas; see Ármann Jakobsson 2005.

[18] 1 Corinthians 11: 1. *Imitatores mei estote, sicut et ego Christi* 'Be ye followers of me, as I also am of Christ'.

[19] The author is here presumably not referring to himself in the plural but speaking on behalf of Þorlákr and his disciples, who may have been the group responsible for the composition of *Þorláks saga*, *Hungrvaka* and *Páls saga*.

[20] There is a parallel in the words of St Jón Ǫgmundarson about Ísleifr Gizurarson, that he would *ávallt geta er ek heyri góðs manns getit* 'always mention [him] when I hear a good man spoken of' (*Jóns saga ins helga*, 183).

[21] This metaphor has a parallel in *Vitæ Patrum*: *Sva fluttu helgir feðr, at hinn merkiligi guds maðr Macharius elskade einna mest allra feðra eydemorkina, þviat hann kannadi hana alla i uthorn* 'the holy fathers related that the most distinguished servant of God, Macharios, loved the desert most of all the fathers as he explored it to its extremities'. In Latin this is *Ita ut etiam ultima et inaccessibilia deserti perscrutatus sit loca*, so that *úthorn* (translated here as 'utmost') is the same as *ultima* (*Heilagra manna søgur* . . . 1877, II 470).

[22] St Isidore (born *c.*560, d. 4 April 636), metropolitan of Seville from 600. His brother Leander (540–600) held office before him (from 594). Isidore presided over

two church councils in his lifetime (619 in Seville and 633 in Toledo). Seventeen works have been attributed to him, of which *Etymologiarum sive originum libri* or the *Etymologiae* (twenty volumes) is best known. Isidore was very influential in the Middle Ages, although he was neither canonised until 1598 nor officially declared a doctor of the church until 1722. Helgi Guðmundsson has identified the quotation as being from Isidore's *Sentences* II.1.11: *Utile est multa scire et recta vivere. Quod si utrumque non valemus, melius est ute bene Vivendi stadium quam multa sciendi sequamur* (*Sancti Isidori Hispalensis Sententiarum libri tres* 1850, 601; Helgi Guðmundsson 2003, 237–38).

[23] On this education see Ásdís Egilsdóttir 1994.

[24] Bjǫrn Gilsson was bishop at Hólar at the time, and would have been expected to carry out the duties of the bishop of Skálaholt in the absence of an elect there. After Magnús Einarsson's death Hallr Teitsson, the grandson of the first bishop Ísleifr of Skálaholt, was elected bishop, but he died abroad in 1150 and does not seem to have received papal approval in spite of his great language skills (*Hungrvaka*, 34). He was married, a chieftain (*goði*) and in his sixties when elected, so it might be argued that in electing him, the Icelanders were testing the patience of the Church with their candidates. Bjǫrn himself is probably the least-known Icelandic bishop of the Commonwealth age. He is believed to be a descendant of Einarr of Þverá, brother of Guðmundr inn ríki. Bjǫrn's sister was Þórný, wife of Jón Sigmundarson of Svínafell. His brother was also Bjǫrn, abbot at Þverá (the second Icelandic monastery, founded partly from Bjǫrn's own estate). His mother was Þórunn, daughter of Bjǫrn, son of Þorfinnr karlsefni. On his mother's side Bjǫrn is related to the bishops Þorlákr Runólfsson and Brandr Sæmundarson. Bjǫrn is mentioned in *Hungrvaka*, *Jóns saga helga* and *Guðmundar saga*. He studied with Teitr Ísleifsson in Haukadalr and later with Bishop Jón at Hólar. He was bishop from 1147 and died on 20 October 1162. In the *Prestssaga* of Guðmundr Arason he is said to have indirectly pointed to Brandr Sæmundarson as his successor. When Jón Ǫgmundarson is made saint, Bjǫrn's relics are translated as well. In *Rannveigar leiðsla* in *Guðmundar saga* it is mentioned that all the bishops are saintly, but Bjǫrn comes fourth in saintliness (after Þorlákr, Jón and Ísleifr). We may infer that Bjǫrn was a devout bishop, and perhaps unmarried (his descendants are not known). Ólafur Halldórsson has suggested that a prophecy that Guðríðr Þorbjarnardóttir's descendants will be mature, bright, sweet and with a good scent is an indirect reference to Bishop Bjǫrn; he believes that a *vita* of Bjǫrn may have been under composition around 1200 (Ólafur Halldórsson 1985, 384–86).

[25] Although exemptions from the age requirement of thirty for priestly ordination appear common, Þorlákr's youth (seventeen or eighteen, perhaps) must be considered highly unusual.

[26] The profitable parishes have not been identified but were probably in the south of Iceland.

[27] The author tends to be somewhat opaque in his criticism of his contemporaries.

[28] Psalms 131: 9–10. *Sacerdotes tui induantur iustitiam et sancti tui exsultent—propter David servum tuum nun avertas faciem Christi tui* 'Let thy priests

be clothed with justice and let thy saints rejoice—For thy servant David's sake, turn not away the face of thy anointed'. This is a somewhat indirect quotation.

²⁹ It is likely that Þorlákr studied at one of the distinguished cathedral schools in Paris, perhaps the school of St Genevieve or the school of St Victor. The latter had several Scandinavian pupils at the same time who later became important church leaders, such as Eiríkr Ívarsson and Þórir Guðmundsson, both archbishops at Niðaróss around 1200. Lincoln also had a cathedral, founded in 1072 (moved from Dorchester at the instigation of King William I); it had previously been an important Viking stronghold. In the twelfth century Lincoln was the largest diocese in England and had important connections with Paris. Alexander (1093–1148) had been bishop of Lincoln just before Þorlákr arrived; a great Cistercian scholar, to whom Geoffrey of Monmouth dedicated *Prophetiae Merlini* (later translated into Icelandic by Gunnlaugr Leifsson). In the thirteenth century the renowned scholar Robert Grosseteste was bishop at Lincoln.

³⁰ These foster-brothers are presumably his fellow students with Eyjólfr Sæmundarson.

³¹ The name Eyvǫr is in Þorlákr's family (his grandmother was Eyvǫr Leifsdóttir) but nothing is known of this sister and her conduct. Ragnheiðr, however, became the concubine of Jón Loptsson, evidently to Þorlákr's displeasure. *Oddaverja þáttr* relates how it became necessary for him to interfere in their affairs (*Þorláks saga*, 175, 180). Páll Jónsson, Þorlákr's successor, is the subject of *Páls saga byskups*.

³² In 1190 Archbishop Eiríkr Ívarsson of Niðaróss wrote to the Pope and complained that Bishop Njáll of Stavanger (1188–1207) had married a woman who was already married, i.e. a widow. However, Eiríkr did not mention the marriages of priests in his letter of admonition to the Icelandic chieftains from 1180, although he did refer to the concubines of Jón Loptsson and Gizurr Hallsson (*Norske middelalderdokumenter* 1973, 62–67; *DI*, I 260–64).

³³ According to *Kristni saga* and *Flateyjarbók* (*Kristni þáttr*), Skeggi Ásgautsson lived in Háfr around 1000. He was the son of Ásgautr Ásmundsson who was descended from the Irish king Cerbhall. Skeggi's mother was Þórdís, daughter of Þorkell bjálfi who settled all the area between Ragná and Þjórsá and lived in Háfr. Skeggi's son Þorvaldr, already grown up in 1000, married Koltorfa, sister of Hjalti Skeggjason. It is not known who lived in Háfr after Skeggi and Þorvaldr, and thus the identity of this widow remains unclear (*Kristni saga*, 31; *Flateyjarbók* 1944–45, I 491).

³⁴ Luke 14: 11. *Qui se humiliat, exaltabitur* 'he that humbleth himself shall be exalted'. This is a very popular citation in medieval Icelandic literature (Kirby 1976–80, I 252–53).

³⁵ Matthew 11: 29. *Discite a me, quia mitis sum et humilis corde; et invenietis requiem animabus vestris* 'learn of me, because I am meek, and humble of heart, and you shall find rest to your souls'. This passage is also frequently used in Icelandic texts of the Middle Ages (Kirby 1976–80, I 164–65).

³⁶ Ketill fíflski 'the Foolish', presumably so called by the heathens because he was a Christian (cf. Finnur Jónsson 1907, 250), son of Jórunn manvitsbrekka (the meaning of this nickname is unclear), first lived at Kirkjubœr at Síða, as it

says in *Landnámabók*: 'The *papar* had lived there before and no heathen could live there' (*Landnámabók*, 324–25). Ketill is mentioned as both one of the noble settlers and a Christian in *Landnámabók*. His son was Ásbjǫrn, father of Þorsteinn, father of Surtr, who lived in Kirkjubœr around 1000 and is mentioned in *Óláfs saga Tryggvasonar en mesta* ('these men were all Christians', *Óláfs saga Tryggvasonar en mesta* 1958–2000, II 156). Later there was a nunnery at Kirkjubœr, founded in 1186. Bjarnheðinn was a descendant of Þorgeirr hǫggvinkinni, a settler who lived at Hǫfn; he is named in the *Prestatal* of 1143 and is likely to be the Bjarnheðinn who founded a church at Keldugnúpr at Síða around 1150 (*DI*, I 200–01). According to the annals he died in 1173 or 1174, and *Hungrvaka* lists him and his brother Beinir who died in the reign of Bishop Klœngr (*Islandske Annaler indtil 1578* 1888, 21 (*Annales reseniani*), 61 (*Henrik Høyers Annaler*), 118 (*Annales regii*), 323 (*Gottskalks Annaler*); (*Flateyjarbók* 1944–45, IV 304; *Oddaverjaannáll*, 134; *Hungrvaka*, 41). Bjarnheðinn is likely to have been about twenty years older than Þorlákr.

[37] In the original there is alliteration within each pair of adjectives.

[38] The word used is *vistarfar*, which suggests that Þorlákr is a servant of Bjarnheðinn; this may be revealing about the status of priests in the twelfth century.

[39] Matthew 11: 30. *Iugum enim meum suave est et onus meum leve* 'For my yoke is sweet and my burden light'.

[40] Matthew 5: 14. *Vos estis lux mundi* 'You are the light of the world'.

[41] The path of mercy is *Líknarbraut*, which also serves as the name of a late-thirteenth-century poem of the Cross, in the skaldic *dróttkvætt* metre.

[42] Matthew 5: 16. *Sic luceat lux vestra coram hominibus, ut videant opera vestra bona, et glorificent patrem vestrum, qui in caelis est* 'So let your light shine before men, that they may see your good works, and glorify your Father who is in heaven'.

[43] Acts 4: 32. *Multitudinis autem credentium erat cor unum et anima una: nec quisquam eorum quæ possidebat, aliquid suum esse dicebat, sed erant illis omnia communia* 'And the multitude of believers had but one heart and one soul. Neither did any one say that aught of the things which he possessed was his own: but all things were common unto them'.

[44] Þorkell son of Geirr, son of Þorkell læknir 'the Healer', son of Geirr (d. 1187).

[45] *frændr* could also mean 'friends' in this context, rather than (distant) relatives.

[46] That is, to become a canon regular and live under the monastic rule.

[47] Luke 14: 33. *Sic ergo omnis ex vobis, qui non renuntiat omnibus quæ possidet, non potest meus esse discipulus* 'So likewise every one of you that doth not renounce all that he possesseth cannot be my disciple'.

[48] The monastery at Þykkvabœr in Ver was established in 1168, with Þorlákr as its first abbot in 1170, then Guðmundr Bjálfason. It was thus established two years before Archbishop Eysteinn founded the first Augustinian monastery in Norway in 1170.

[49] Þorlákr was presumably 37 years old when he was consecrated an abbot in 1170. Þorlákr arrived in Kirkjubœr in 1162 and Ver in 1168, first as prior and then as abbot, as confirmed by the lists of abbots by Haukr Erlendsson and in *Rímbegla* (*DI*, III 29, 312). As an abbot Þorlákr was independent of the bishop.

The community of canons at Þykkvabœr was the first to be established in Iceland (followed by Helgafell, Viðey and Möðruvellir) and the establishment of such communities is in line with the Scandinavian fashion of the time.

[50] Matthew 18: 20. *Ubi enim sunt duo vel tres congregati in nomine meo, ibi sum in medio eorum* 'For where there are two or three gathered together in my name, there am I in the midst of them'.

[51] Restriction of travelling is one of the pillars of the Benedictine order, and of the Augustinian order that was modelled on it. Þorlákr may have been one of the first abbots to enforce this ban.

[52] I Thessalonians 5: 17–18. *Sine intermissione orate, in omnibus gratias agite* 'Pray without ceasing, in all things give thanks'.

[53] Matthew 24: 13. *Qui autem perseveraverit usque in finem, hic salvus erit* 'But he that shall persevere to the end, he shall be saved'. This passage is frequently quoted in medieval Icelandic (Kirby 1976–80, I 186–87).

[54] I Corinthians 15: 33. *Corrumpunt mores bonos colloquia mala* 'Evil communications corrupt good manners'.

[55] Psalm 38: 2–3. *Cum consisteret peccator adversum me, obmutui, et humiliatus sum, et silvi a bonis* 'when the sinner stood against me, I was dumb, and was humbled, and kept silence from good things'. The saga's translation of this verse is somewhat loose.

[56] The author adheres to the principle that all miracles come from God; even the most powerful saints cannot help except according to God's will.

[57] cf. Ecclesiastes 11: 28.

[58] A similar expression is used in *Páls saga byskups*, 315

[59] Literally, *orpinn* 'bent'.

[60] The archbishop's permission is published in *DI*, I 218–23. It was unusual to elect a new bishop while the old one was alive. In *Hungrvaka,* when in 1118 Gizurr Ísleifsson has had Þorlákr Runólfsson elected in his stead, it is apparent that Archbishop Qzurr is unwilling to *setja hǫfuð á hǫfuð ofan* 'put a head above a head', finally consecrating Þorlákr not to Skálaholt but to Reykjaholt (*Hungrvaka*, 23–24). When Klœngr asks Eysteinn to do the same, it seems to be no longer a problem.

[61] That is, to be consecrated in Niðarós.

[62] Qgmundr Kálfsson was abbot in Flateyjarklaustr, later at Helgafell. Nothing is known of his ancestry. He was drowned in 1187 or 1188. The Augustinian monastery on Flatey was founded in 1172 under the leadership of Qgmundr who donated his property to it (*DI*, I 280–82). He most likely bought Helgafell in 1184 and was the only abbot in that monastery. Qgmundr was less senior than Þorlákr and was probably only a candidate through his wealth and connections. Páll Sǫlvason was descended from the notable settler Hrólfr Kjallaksson, his grandfather was Magnús Þórðarson in Reykjaholt who is mentioned in *Kristni saga* and his paternal aunt was Bishop Magnús Einarsson's stepmother. His father was killed in 1128 or 1129. His wife was Þorbjǫrg Bjarnadóttir (d. 1181), and both feature prominently in *Sturlu saga*. They had four children. Þorbjǫrg's sister was the wife of Bishop Brandr Sæmundsson. Páll was already a priest in 1143 and was a man of some importance in 1148, when Bishop Magnús perished in a fire. According to *Sturlu*

Notes

saga he was wealthy and, unlike Sturla, well connected with most of the notable magnates of Iceland. He died in 1185. Páll was in all likelihood in his sixties in 1174 and that may be the main reason why his powerful friends did not get him the job (see Ármann Jakobsson 2000, 180–81). He interprets a dream about Þorlákr's holiness (ch. 17). See further *Kristni saga* 42; *Sturlunga saga*, I 103–14.

[63] Conceit (*sjálfvirðing*) presumably refers to *superbia*, the most serious of the deadly sins.

[64] This happened in 1174, when he was forty.

[65] Þorlákr's election is hardly surprising considering that he had played a leading role in the foundation of the first Augustinian monastery in Iceland and had probably worked closely with Klœngr and was thus in touch with the church reform of the time. It may also have helped him that he was raised in Oddi and was thus connected to the most powerful families in the diocese during the eleventh and twelfth centuries, the Oddi and Haukadalr clans.

[66] Gizurr lived close to Skálaholt, in Haukadalr. Later he took up residence in Skálaholt (see ch. 80), as is told even more clearly in the B-version (*Þorláks saga* 185; *Sturlunga saga*, I 139–40; *Páls saga byskups*, 300). In the Latin fragments of *Þorláks saga*, Jón Loptsson is referred to as *princeps patriae*, which may reflect his role as an unofficial 'king of Iceland' in some thirteenth-century saga texts (*Latínubrot um Þorlák byskup*, 349; Ármann Jakobsson 1997, 295–98).

[67] *Hungrvaka* depicts Klœngr as recklessly extravagant, and insinuates that he invited so many to the consecration of the new church at Skálaholt that there were seventy for breakfast the following day and the food ran out (*Hungrvaka*, 35–38).

[68] Presumably the recipients of Klœngr's excessive hospitality.

[69] These hostilities seem to be referred to in the letters of Archbishop Eysteinn (*DI*, I 223). They may include the dispute between Helgi Skaptason and the Norwegian Brennu-Páll in 1175, which is mentioned in passing in the *Prestssaga Guðmundar Arasonar* (*Sturlunga saga*, I 124–25).

[70] Klœngr died on 28 February 1176.

[71] This might be from a reading for either of the two feast days of St Paul (25 January and 30 June), or perhaps the subject of a homily preached on one of those days. For January the lesson should be Acts 9, for June Gal. 1: 11–20 and Matthew 10: 16–22, but these do not include a passage of that kind. On the other hand, in Philippians 1: 28 the saint says 'in nothing be terrified by your adversaries' (*et in nullo terreamini ab adversariis*). Cf. Hebrews 13: 6.

[72] The Latin term *electus* is used in the original. According to Magnús Már Lárusson, Þorlákr as an *electus* had more authority than a mere bishop-elect (*postulatus*): 'hann hafi haft jus in re in spiritualibus et temporalibus, sem postulatus, sá tilnefndi, hafði ekki, er Þorlákur tók við staðarforráðum' (Magnús Már Lárusson 1956 [1967], 55).

[73] Eysteinn Erlendsson was a little older than Þorlákr, probably born around 1120. His father, Erlendr hímaldi Jónasson, was related to King Magnús berfœttr (d. 1103). Erlendr's grandfather was the Icelander Úlfr Óspaksson, *stallari* 'marshal' to King Haraldr harðráði, who was married to Jórunn, daughter of Þorbergr Árnason and granddaughter of the notable magnate Erlingr Skjálgsson. Eysteinn

studied abroad, probably in England and France. He was chancellor to King Ingi, chaplain and treasurer, before he became archbishop in 1157, selected by the king himself. He had also been priest of the church in Konungahella. Eysteinn went to Rome to be consecrated and stayed in the abbey of St Victor (where Þorlákr may have been at the time). He was consecrated on 4 February 1161. An able administrator, Eysteinn managed to make an alliance with King Magnús and Jarl Erlingr, and to crown King Magnús as the vassal of St Óláfr in 1163 and 1164. He founded Augustinian monasteries and worked on a new ecclesiastical law in Norway. When King Sverrir took power, Eysteinn fell into disfavour and was in exile in England 1180–83. Later he made peace with Sverrir and died 26 January 1188. His successor, Eiríkr, was probably more ardent in his pursuit of church autonomy. Eysteinn was proclaimed a saint by a Norwegian synod in 1229 but never achieved general recognition.

[74] King Magnús Erlingsson ruled Norway from 1161 to 1184, his father Jarl Erlingr acting as unofficial regent until he was killed in 1179. Magnús had sworn allegiance to St Óláfr as the 'rex perpetuus Norvegiae', and, as the Church was acting for the saint, he was technically her vassal. However, as this passage indicates, the king and his father were still very much in charge.

[75] Psalm 117: 9. *Bonum est sperare in Domino, quam sperare in principibus* 'It is good to trust in the Lord, rather than to trust in princes'.

[76] 1 Peter 2: 17. *Deum timete, regem honorificate* 'Fear God, honour the king'. See also *Óláfs saga Tryggvasonar eptir Odd munk Snorrason* 2006, 126.

[77] The word *vingunarsvipr* seems to indicate that there was no genuine friendship between the king and jarl and Þorlákr. The insinuation may stem from the admiration shown in the saga for King Sverrir. The quotation from Sverrir may have come from oral tradition (perhaps passed on by his biographer, Abbot Karl Jónsson of Þingeyrar) or from a letter now lost. It is unclear why King Magnús and Jarl Erlingr should object to Þorlákr, but it may be related to the aforementioned quarrel between Icelanders and Norwegians.

[78] Pope Alexander III ruled from 7 September 1159 to his death, 30 August 1181. He was Orlando Bandinelli from Siena, born *c*.1100. He was a teacher of law in Bologna (1139–42) and then canon in Pisa, was created cardinal deacon in 1150 and cardinal priest in 1151. In 1153 he became papal chancellor and the main advisor to Pope Adrian IV (the English pope), was considered a friend of Normandy and opposed to Emperor Frederick I Barbarossa. In 1159 he was chosen as pope by the enemies of the emperor but the minority chose Ottavian Monticelli (antipope Victor IV) and then three other antipopes (Paschal III, Callistus III and Innocent III), throughout his reign. His papacy marks an intensification of the hostilities between emperor and pope. He was compelled to leave Rome twice in his reign, dwelling first in France and then Italy. In 1177 he was finally recognised by Frederick III, in the peace of Venice. Alexander III was the first great lawyer pope, and was for a long while believed to be the author of *Summa Rolandi* (one of the earliest commentaries on the *Decretum Gratiani*) and the *Sententiae Rolandi*. See further Baldwin 1968.

[79] This happened on 2 July, 1178. The feast of Peter and Paul is the 29 June, but Paul is not mentioned here in spite of the saga's numerous quotations of the

Pauline letters. It was probably important to connect events in the *vitae* of church leaders to St Peter as the Pope's predecessor.

[80] Eiríkr Ívarsson was archbishop 1188–1205. He died in 1213. Eiríkr was probably slightly older than Þorlákr (born around 1130). His father was an Icelander, Ívarr skrauthanki, who became bishop in Niðaróss. Eiríkr studied in the abbey of St Victor in the 1150s, where the day of his death (3 May) was observed for a long time. He was bishop of Stavanger in 1171 and close to Archbishop Eysteinn in opposition to King Sverrir. When he became archbishop, hostilities between him and the king soon emerged and he fled the country, staying with Bishop Absalon of Lund from 1191 until after Sverrir had died in 1202, enjoying the support of the Danes. Shortly after going into exile he lost his eyesight, which in *Sverris saga* is interpreted as a sign of divine disfavour for his opposition to the king. In 1190 he wrote a letter to the pope which led to King Sverrir's excommunication in 1194. Eiríkr had originally supported the Baglar but returned home as a royalist, supported King Ingi against Hákon galinn in 1204 and was present at their settlement in 1212 (*Sverris saga* 2007).

[81] Páll was bishop of Bergen from 1156 to his death in 1194. He had previously been chaplain to King Eysteinn Haraldsson, who was instrumental in making him a bishop. Since Páll died the year after St Þorlákr, the statement of their lifelong friendship is hardly an exaggeration.

[82] Eysteinn had consecrated between four and six bishops before Þorlákr: Eiríkr Ívarsson (Stavanger 1172), who was presumably the most notable, Helgi (Oslo 1169/1170), Brandr Sæmundarson (Hólar 1163), Ormarr or Ragnarr (Hamar *c.*1164), Vilhjálmr (Kirkjuvágr, Orkney, 1168) and Hrói or Sveinn (the Faroes, 1162). As none of the others became a saint, Þorlákr may indeed be considered the foremost. The archbishop of Niðaróss had ten bishops under him, four in Norway (Viken, Stavanger, Hamar and Bergen), two in Iceland (Skálaholt and Hólar) and one each in the Faroes, Greenland, Orkney and the Hebrides. For background, see Bagge 2003.

[83] These adjectives alliterate in the Icelandic; many thanks to Alison Finlay for her translation of this sentence. Cf. Titus 1: 7–9. *Oportet enim episcopum sine crimine esse, sicut Dei dispensatorem, non superbum, non iracundum, non vinolentum, non percussorem, non turpis lucri cupidum; sed hospitalem, benignum, sobrium, iustum, sanctum, continentem, amplectentem eum qui secundum doctrinam est, fidelem sermonem ut potens sit exhortari, in doctrina sana, et eos qui contradicunt, arguere* 'For a bishop must be without crime, as the steward of God: not proud, not subject to anger, nor given to wine, no striker, not greedy of filthy lucre, but given to hospitality, gentle, sober, just, holy, continent, embracing that faithful word which is according to doctrine, that he may be able to exhort in sound doctrine and to convince the gainsayers'.

[84] This would be 9 August. St Laurence was martyred on 10 August, AD 258.

[85] II Timothy 4: 2. *Argue, obsecra, increpa in omni patientia et doctrina* 'reprove, entreat, rebuke in all patience and doctrine'.

[86] He was probably aided in this by Gizurr Hallsson, who later took up residence at Skálaholt, or Gizurr's son, Þorvaldr, who helped him with the finances on his

deathbed. Þorlákr was probably compelled to pursue a stringent financial policy after the reckless spending of Bishop Klœngr (cf. chs 9 and 10).

[87] The saga author is here drawing an implicit contrast with Bishop Klœngr's mismanagement.

[88] Psalm 118: 103. *Quam dulcia faucibus meis eloquia tua, super mel ori meo!* 'How sweet are thy words to my palate! more than honey to my mouth'. The phrase occurs in *Vitus saga* and *Homiliu-bók* (*Heilagra manna søgur* . . . 1877, 328; *Homiliu-bók* . . . 1872, 186).

[89] Matthew 24: 46. *Beatus ille servus, quem cum venerit dominus eius, invenerit sic facientem* 'Blessed is that servant, who when his lord shall come he shall find so doing'; cf. Matt. 12:37. *Beati servi illi, quos cum venerit dominus, invenerit vigilantes.*

[90] Matthew 24: 42. *Vigilate ergo, quia nescitis qua hora Dominus vester venturus sit* 'Watch ye therefore, because you know not what hour your Lord will come'.

[91] cf. Matthew 24: 47. *Amen dico vobis, quoniam super omnia bona sua constituet eum* 'Amen I say to you: he shall place him over all his goods'.

[92] cf. Matthew 17: 21. *Hoc genus non eiicitur, nisi in oratione et ieiunio* 'But this kind is not cast out but by prayer and fasting'.

[93] Matthew 5: 5. *Beati qui lugent, quoniam ipsi consolabuntur* 'Blessed are they that mourn: for they shall be comforted'. This phrase is also found in *Homiliu-bók* . . . 1872, 49.

[94] John 16: 20. *Tristitia vestra vertetur in gaudium* 'your sorrow shall be turned into joy'.

[95] cf. James 1: 20. *Ira enim viri iustitiam Dei non operatur* 'For the anger of man worketh not the justice of God'.

[96] Romans 12: 21. *Noli vinci a malo, sed vince in bono malum* 'Be not overcome by evil but overcome evil by good'.

[97] Revelation 1: 3. *Beatus qui legit et audit verba prophetiae huius et servat ea quae in ea scripta sunt* 'Blessed is he that readeth and heareth the words of this prophecy: and keepeth those things which are written in it'.

[98] Psalm 33: 11. *Venite, filii, audite me: timorem domini docebo vos* 'Come, children, hearken to me: I will teach you the fear of the Lord'.

[99] II Corinthians 1: 13. *Non enim alia scribimus vobis quam quae legistis et cognovistis* 'For we write no other things to you than what you have read and known'. The Icelandic translation is somewhat liberal.

[100] cf. James 5: 16. *Multum enim valet deprecatio iusti assidua* 'For the continual prayer of a just man availeth much'.

[101] Matthew 5: 4. *Beati mites (quoniam ipsi possidebunt terram)* 'Blessed are the meek, for they shall possess the land'. Here, 'eternally' is added.

[102] The original reads 'hve mjǫk þat er kallat at á hirti ríði'. This is clearly an idiom, as in modern Icelandic *áríðandi* and in the English 'much rides on this'. The deer (*hjǫrtr*) is obviously a swift animal.

[103] The descending order of the numbers seems strange, but these are holy numbers, especially seven (the days of the week, the cardinal virtues) and twelve (the months of the year, the number of the apostles). The number nine seems to

have less relevance to the Christian faith, although it is an old sacred number for Græco-Roman culture and the pagan North (see Laugesen 1959).

[104] Although Þorlákr, like many other saints and bishops, follows Christ's example in this, Christ in fact dried his disciples' feet with a towel (John 13: 2–5): it was Mary, the sister of Martha, who dried Christ's feet with her hair after anointing them with oil (John 12: 3).

[105] John 13: 15. *Exempli enim dedi vobis, ut que madmodum ego feci vobis, ita et vos faciatis* 'For I have given you an example, that as I have done to you, so you do also'.

[106] Matthew 6: 3. *Te autem faciente eleemosynam, nesciat sinistra tua, quid faciat dextera tua* 'But when thou dost alms, let not thy left hand know what thy right hand doth'. This is the proper way to give alms, according to Christ himself and Matthew.

[107] The negative follows an emendation by Guðbrandur Vigfússon, which seems more logical than the manuscript reading (*Origines Islandicae* . . . 1905, 485).

[108] This seems to refer to events described in *Oddaverja þáttr*.

[109] Ezekiel 33: 11. *Nolo mortem peccatoris sed ut inpius convertatur et vivat* 'I desire not the death of the wicked, but that the wicked turn from his way, and live'. This is a very popular citation in medieval Iceland (Kirby 1976–80, I 109–10).

[110] Either the same, or Ezekiel 18:27: *Et cum averterit se impius ab impietate sua, quam operatus est et fecerit iudicium et iustitiam, ipse animam suam vivificabit* 'And when the wicked turneth himself away from his wickedness, which he hath wrought, and doeth judgment, and justice: he shall save his soul alive'.

[111] Matthew 18: 17. *Si autem ecclesiam non audierit, sit tibi sicut ethnicus et publicanus* 'And if he will not hear the church, let him be to thee as the heathen and publican'.

[112] Matthew 5: 9. *Beati pacifici, quoniam filii Dei vocabuntur* 'Blessed are the peacemakers: for they shall be called the children of God'. Another quotation from the Sermon on the Mount, cf. notes 40 and 42.

[113] This could be a reference to 1 Cor. 9: 22 ('To the weak I became weak, that I might gain the weak. I became all things to all men, that I might save all') or to 2 Cor. 11, where Paul describes his sufferings.

[114] The 'unions of men' (*ráð manna*) seems to refer principally to marriages between men and women, although it might also refer to the other ties created by these marriages.

[115] This sentence is extremely convoluted in the original.

[116] cf. Psalm 83: 12. *Misericordiam et veritatem diligit Deus, gratiam et gloriam dabit Dominus* 'For God loveth mercy and truth: the Lord will give grace and glory'.

[117] Guðmundr Bjálfason was abbot in Þykkvabœr (Ver) from 1178 to his death in 1197. He is mentioned also in *Páls saga byskups* (331), but little is known about his family or background.

[118] See ch. 9.

[119] St Ambrose's Day is 7 December. His legend was translated into Icelandic and he was co-patron of the Church at Hǫfði in Hǫfðahverfi. St Cecilia's Day is 22 November. She was patron saint of churches in Húsafell, Nes in Aðaldalr and

Saurbœr in Eyjafjǫrðr, but a second patron in Otradalr. Her legend also existed in Icelandic. St. Agnes' Day is 21 January. Her legend exists in three Icelandic versions and she was a joint patron of Þerney and Bœr in Borgarfjǫrðr. The Feasts of the Apostles were: Peter (and Paul) 29 June, Andrew 30 November, James 25 July, John 6 May and 27 December, Thomas 3 July and 21 December, Matthew 21 September, Matthias 24 or 25 February, Bartholomew (or Nathaniel) 24 August, Philip and James the Lesser shared 1 May, St Jude (Thaddeus) and Simon shared 28 October. All the apostles had legends in Icelandic but their popularity as patron saints of Icelandic churches varied. The Mass of St Nicholas was 6 December. More than forty churches were consecrated to him (alone or with others) and several versions of his legend existed (Cormack 1994, 74–165; *Heilagra manna søgur* . . . 1877, I 15–22 (*Agnesar Saga Meyjar*), 28–51 (*Ambrosius Saga Byskups*), 276–97 (*Ceciliu Saga Meyjar*)). The sagas of the apostles are edited in *Postola sögur* . . . 1874.

[120] Fridays which were not feast days were called *rúmhelgr* and one meal apparently sufficed.

[121] *white food*: dairy products.

[122] If Christmas fell on a Friday the feast would take precedence over the discipline of fasting, so Þorlákr should have been eating meat that day whether he was ill or not, and yet the author insists on his illness as an explanation. Christmas Day would have fallen on a Friday in 1181, 1187 and 1192.

[123] Þorlákr's own parents had separated on account of their poverty, so there is a personal angle to this innovation.

[124] Among these unnamed men is obviously Jón Loptsson, who kept Þorlákr's sister as his concubine with his wife still living, as everyone in the original audience would have realised. The saga often chooses not to mention names. It is unlikely that this is done to spare Jón Loptsson or Páll Jónsson, his son and Þorlákr's successor (conceived in such an unlawful marriage), since everyone would have known of this in any case and the reference is clear enough. It is more likely that the author believes that the general is more important than the individual and thus decides never to mention names of sinners.

[125] Clearly, worldly longings are not suitable for a saint.

[126] The Ember Days are four separate sets of three days within the same week (the Wednesday, Friday and Saturday) set aside for fasting and prayer. The Ember weeks are between the first and second Sundays of Lent, between Pentecost and Trinity Sunday, the week beginning on the Sunday after Holy Cross Day (14 September), and the week between the third and fourth Sundays of Advent. The rule that fixes the ordination of clergy in the Ember weeks is traditionally associated with Pope Gelasius I (d. 496). The Icelandic name *imbrudagar* seems to be derived from Old English.

[127] These tokens functioned much as written references in support of job applications do now.

[128] The word used is *bóksǫgur* which presumably means written legends.

[129] Compare the numbers of the men whose feet Þorlákr washed, n. 103 above.

[130] II Corinthians 12: 9. *Et dixit mihi: sufficit tibi gratia mea, nam virtus in infirmitate perficitur* 'And he said to me: My grace is sufficient for thee, for power

is made perfect in infirmity'. The term used in Icelandic is *sjúkleikr* 'illness' (see Kirby 1976–80, II 379).

[131] The Apostles' Creed and the Lord's Prayer ('Our Father. . .').

[132] *Iesu nostra redemptio*: This hymn dates to the seventh or eighth century. The second line is usually *amor et desiderium* but other versions exist: the second line can be *amor er vita pauperum* etc.

[133] Eight hymns are attributed to Pope Gregory the Great (d. 604) by Benedictine monks. Of those, *Nocte surgentes vigilemus* and *Ecce jam noctis tenuatur umbra* are as a rule sung every morning but *Primo dierum omnium* is also a morning hymn.

[134] Psalm 1: 1–2. *Beatus vir qui non abiit in consilio impiorum et in via peccatorum non stetit et in cathedra pestilentiae non sedit, sed in lege Domini voluntas eius* 'Blessed is the man who hath not walked in the counsel of the ungodly, nor stood in the way of sinners, nor sat in the chair of pestilence, but his will is in the law of the Lord'.

[135] This is the Little Office of the Blessed Virgin Mary, a monastic devotion which may have originated in the eighth century but came into general use in the tenth century. In the twelfth century, some Augustinian Canons prescribed the Little Office in addition to the eight hours of the Divine Office and later it became obligatory for all clergy.

[136] His usual singing would be what Þorlákr sings every day, which seems to indicate that he habitually finished the psalter in three days, fifty psalms each day, in addition to the psalms which are part of the offices he recites each day.

[137] *Gloria patri*: An ancient hymn, used both in the East and in the West from the early Middle Ages and existing in various versions. The standard Latin version is: *Gloria patri et Filio et Spiritui Sancto: Sicut erat in principio, et nunc, et semper, et in saecula saeculorum*. It was customary to sing *Gloria patri* after each psalm.

[138] Psalm 56: 2. *Miserere mei Deus, miserere mei, quoniam in te confidit anima mea* 'Have mercy on me, O God, have mercy on me; while my soul puts its trust in thee'. This psalm is quoted by King Sverrir after the death of King Magnús Erlingsson in 1184 (*Sverris saga* 2007, 152).

[139] *Salvum fac pater et Domine*: Psalm 27: 9: *Salvum fac populum tuum, Domine, et benedic haereditati tuae. Et rege eos et extolle illos usque in aeternum* 'Save, O Lord, thy people, and bless thy inheritance, and rule them and exalt them for ever'. This verse is used in the *Te Deum* and in the Hours, which may be the case in this instance.

[140] Psalm 19: 3. *Mittat tibi auxilium de sancto et de Sion roboret te* 'May he send thee help from the sanctuary: and defend thee out of Sion'. This is much used in prayers. There is no similar prayer of Solomon in the Vulgate.

[141] Psalm 33: 1. *Benedicam dominum in omni tempore semper laus eius in ore meo* 'I will bless the Lord at all times, his praise shall be always in my mouth'.

[142] Psalm 14: 1–2. *Domine quis habitabit in tabernaculo tuo? aut quis requiescet in monte sancto tuo? Qui ingreditur sine macula et operatur iustitiam* 'Lord, who shall dwell in thy tabernacle? or who shall rest in thy holy hill? He that walketh without blemish, and worketh justice'.

Notes

¹⁴³ It is unclear what those games were and why they were more antipathetical to the saint than stories or music.

¹⁴⁴ Bishop St Martin of Tours (c.315–97), one of the most notable Western European saints of the early Middle Ages and one of the first who was neither a martyr nor a hermit, i.e. one of the foremost representatives of the *vita activa*. He enjoyed respect in twelfth- and thirteenth-century Iceland, more among the learned than the general public, and is mentioned in both *Jóns saga helga* and *Guðmundar saga*. He is often regarded as the father of monastic life in France. His popularity in the North may be connected to the links various Norse church leaders had with France and England (*Jóns saga ins helga*, 222–23, 297, 301; *Guðmundar saga* A, 120; *Brot úr miðsögu Guðmundar*, 594). On St Martin see, e.g., Stancliffe 1983.

¹⁴⁵ This is the same Páll who contended with Þorlákr for the office of bishop.

¹⁴⁶ Although Þorlákr led the life of an active saint (*vita activa*), given his role as a church official, his life is nevertheless presented as essentially one of solitude and abstinence (*vita contemplativa*). This is not unusual; most biographers of active saints stress their self-denial and ascetic habits.

¹⁴⁷ Gizurr Hallsson, along with Jón Loptsson, had been admonished by the archbishop of Niðarós for having 'two wives' (see Introduction, pp. xv and xvii, and notes to the text 31, 32 and 124). One can assume that when he moved to Skálaholt, he had repented and given up one or both wives.

¹⁴⁸ Bishop Brandr Sæmundarson was of the Oddi family and was also related to Þorlákr Runólfsson, bishop at Skálaholt. He and Páll Sǫlvason, who competed against Þorlákr in 1174, were married to sisters. Brandr was probably born around 1110. He was consecrated to the see of Hólar in 1163 and died in 1201, and figures prominently in *Sturlunga saga*, *Jóns saga helga* and *Guðmundar saga*. Two of his greatest accomplishments were achieved in his extreme old age, the translation of St Þorlákr in 1198 and the translation of St Jón of Hólar in 1200 (*Sturlunga saga*, I 53, 55, 86, 105–211, 238, 240; II 87; *Jóns saga ins helga*, 242, 254–56, 269–79, 288, 302–04, 308–09; *Guðmundar saga* A; *Brot úr miðsögu Guðmundar*, 561).

¹⁴⁹ Páll was bishop of Skálaholt from 1195 to 1211, he was the son of Jón Loptsson and Þorlákr's sister Ragnheiðr. *Páls saga* relates that he was buried at Skálaholt in a stone coffin (*Páls saga byskups*, 306). This coffin was dug up in 1954 (Sveinbjörn Rafnsson 1993, 123–27; Eldjárn 1988).

¹⁵⁰ Ormr Eyjólfsson also figures in the B-version of the saga where it is related that after Þorlákr's death he dwelt with Bishop Brandr of Hólar (*Þorláks saga*, 178–79, 194–95).

¹⁵¹ Psalm 116: 15. *Pretiosa in conspectu Domini mora Sanctorum eius* 'Precious in the sight of the Lord is the death of his saints'.

¹⁵² Þorlákr actually died in 1193, but the author makes the 'correction' on grounds of *computatio Gerlandi* (cf. Introduction).

¹⁵³ *Hungrvaka* states that Gizurr was a great authority on the history of the see of Skálaholt (*Hungrvaka*, 3).

¹⁵⁴ Bishop Brandr Sæmundarson was probably around 80 when Þorlákr died (see note 148 above).

[155] Karl Jónsson was abbot of Þingeyrar from 1169–1207 (except for a break in the years 1181–87). He died in 1212 or 1213. Karl is the author of some or all of *Sverris saga* (see Þorleifur Hauksson 2007, xxii–xxiv, lv–lx).

[156] Þorvaldr the priest is called Þorvaldr lundi 'puffin' in the oldest *Guðmundar saga* but is otherwise unknown. According to *Sturlunga saga* a Þorvarðr Klyppsson lived in Lundr in Reykjardalr, but this is not in the North (and the name, though similar, is not the same) (*Guðmundar saga* A, 91; *Sturlunga saga* I 105, 232–33).

[157] 'Years' follows the B/C-version of the saga, a correction of the A-version's 'nights'.

[158] From this point until the saga's penultimate chapter, the chapters are often more like paragraphs, each describing a new miracle. The numbering is continued for ease of reference.

[159] The original word is *fanntóm* which could be the otherwise unknown word *fanntó* 'speck of snow', cf. *grastó* 'turf of grass'.

[160] It is possible that Bishop Páll's lack of initiative in this matter is stressed because he was closely related to Þorlákr.

[161] That is, Lǫgrétta at Þingvellir.

[162] The Mass of St Peter falls on 29 June.

[163] Tjǫrvi the Leprous is only known from this miracle and presumably was not a magnate. The name has a long history in Iceland but has never been popular.

[164] The *Te Deum* or the Ambrosian hymn is an early Christian hymn of praise, traditionally said to have been sung by Sts Ambrose and Augustine when the former baptised the latter in 387, and was used regularly in thanksgiving on special occasions.

[165] Abbot Jón Loptsson or Ljótsson was abbot of Þykkvabœr in Ver from 1197 (after Guðmundr Bjálfason). This is the cloister that Þorlákr himself founded.

[166] Guðmundr gríss 'piglet' Ámundason was a magnate (*goði*) at Þingvellir and *allsherjargoði* (*goði* of the lineage of Ingólfr the first settler), but ended his life as a monk at Þingeyrar/Þverá. He died on 22 February 1210. Guðmundr was Bishop Páll's brother-in-law, the father-in-law of Þorvaldr Gizurarson, the grandfather of Bishop Árni Þorláksson and the great-grandfather of Bishop Árni Helgason. His son, Magnús, was elected bishop of Skálaholt in 1238 but never consecrated (*Sturlunga saga*, I 51, 53, 60, 140, 237, 239, 267, 396; II *8. ættskrá*).

[167] In spite of his noble lineage, this Sighvatr cannot be identified.

[168] Unas is a rare name, otherwise only known as that of King Sverrir's foster-father (Unás kambari) in the Faroes (*Sverris saga*, 4–5). Nothing else is known about this man.

[169] The boy saint Vitus is also mentioned in *Hungrvaka*. He is an early saint from Italy, a child when he died. It is not clear why he appears here since the disease described does not seem to be one of those for which he was usually invoked (fits, nerve diseases and the bites of dogs and snakes). He is one of only a few foreign saints that perform miracles in Iceland, perhaps because his mass (15 June) was the day of the consecration of Skálaholt cathedral (on Trinity Sunday 1158) (Melsted 1903–30, III 233).

[170] This priest is also mentioned in the miracles of the C-version, but little is known about him (*Jarteinabók Þorláks byskups önnur* 2002, 245).

[171] Although Árni óreiða, Snorri Sturluson's son-in-law, is by far the foremost Árni on contemporary record, the reference is probably to a now unknown man of fair standing.

[172] Ormr lived at Breiðabólstaðr and died in 1218. His daughter Hallveig married Bjǫrn Þorvaldsson, son of Þorvaldr Gizurarson, and later lived with Snorri Sturluson.

[173] A Torfi Guðmundarson, a priest at Sauðafell and later in Hjarðarholt who appears widely in *Sturlunga saga*, seems to have been in the service of Sturla Sighvatsson, but it is not known whether he came from a noble family. A Torfi Þorvarðarson, son of Þorvarðr the priest of Lundr, was of noble extraction, being related to Þórir the rich priest from Deildartunga; the name of his wife is not known, but he came from a family of priests (*Sturlunga saga*, I 300, 313–14, 318, 320, 323, 340–41, 348). Torfi's wife is called Halldóra in a miracle in the B-version (*Þorláks saga*, 213).

[174] Magnús Gizurarson (c.1165–1237) was the son of Gizurr Hallsson, and brother of Þorvaldr and Hallr. He was bishop in Skálaholt from 1216. In *Prestssaga Guðmundar Arasonar* it is said that Þorlákr had much respect for all the sons of Gizurr and fostered Magnús in his youth (before consecrating him as priest), with such success that he became very learned, eloquent and prophetic (*Sturlunga saga*, I 140).

[175] That is, either he could not see further than the reach of his fingers, or he could only make things out by feeling with his hands.

[176] In the B-versions, this happens at Hvítá (presumably Hvítá in Árnesþing) (*Þorláks saga*, 200).

[177] This miracle and many of the ensuing ones are more extensively told in *Jarteinabók Þorláks byskups in forna* (2002, 103–25). Holt undir Eyjafjǫllum was settled by Þorgeirr hǫrzki, son of Bárðr blǫnduhorn from Viggja, who settled the land between Írá and Lambafellsá. His wife was Ásgerðr Asksdóttir who had previously been married to Ófeigr, and their son was Þorgeirr gollnir. The sons of Ásgerðr and Þorgeirr from Hǫrðaland were Þorgrímr the Great and Holta-Þórir, whose sons were Þorleifr the Crow and Skorar-Geirr. This family plays an important part in *Brennu-Njáls saga* where the genealogy is different. In *Jarteinabók Þorláks byskups in forna* the farmer of Holt is called Grímr Jónsson, son of Jón Þorgeirsson, priest of Holt. This Grímr died in 1219 and his son lived at Holt after him until 1283. Grímr's son married the daughter of Ormr of Breiðabólstaðr, brother of Bishop Páll himself (*Jarteinabók Þorláks byskups in forna* 2002, 103–04; *Brennu-Njáls saga* 1954, ættskrá 1. a and b).

[178] A longer and more interesting version of this miracle is in the B-version and in *Jarteinabók Þorláks byskups in forna*, where another woman in the vicinity laughs at this miracle as the wife uses the same treatment that is used for pregnant women; this woman is punished by a severe pain in the eyes, although St Þorlákr also heals that when asked (*Þorláks saga*, 210; *Jarteinabók Þorláks byskups in forna* 2002, 114–59).

[179] This may mean that the child's healed eye was a different colour from the other.

[180] Guðmundr Arason was bishop at Hólar from 1203 to 1237. He was later regarded as a saint himself and is the subject of four sagas (or four versions of one saga, depending on definition), commonly designated A, B, C, D.

[181] Þorleifr Þorleiksson from Hítardalr was extremely old at that time; he was already master of the place in 1148, when Bishop Magnús Einarsson perished in a great fire, cf. *Hungrvaka*, 31–32 (esp. note 7). He died in 1200. Þorleifr's grand-daughter Herdís was the wife of Bishop Páll (*Páls saga*, 297).

[182] This could have been either a gallstone or a kidney-stone. This Þorsteinn may have been Þorsteinn Jónsson of Hvammr, father of Eyjólfur ofsi (d. 1255) and of Ásgrímr who became *riddari* (d. 1285). This Þorsteinn is likely to have been in his teens or twenties in the 1190s.

[183] Uni is a rare name in Iceland after the settlement period although examples can be found in *Landnámabók* 220, 242, 296, 299–301.

[184] Þorsteinn Skeggjason is also mentioned in the C-miracles and *Páls saga*, and is said to be the best smith in Iceland. His line is traced in *Landnámabók*, an indication of the respect he must have enjoyed in the late thirteenth century (*Þorláks saga*, 292; *Páls saga byskups*, 310; *Landnámabók*, 256).

[185] There is a miracle in C in which Þorlákr frees captives (who call on him during a siege of the heathens) in a distant land (*Jarteinabók Þorláks byskups önnur* 2002, 236–37).

BIBLIOGRAPHY AND ABBREVIATIONS

PRIMARY SOURCES: EDITIONS AND TRANSLATIONS

Biskupa sögur 1858–78. Ed. Guðbrandur Vigfússon, Jón Sigurðsson, Þorvaldur Bjarnarson and Eiríkur Jónsson. 2 vols. Copenhagen.
Biskupa sögur II 2002. Ed. Ásdís Egilsdóttir. Íslenzk fornrit XVI, 101–40.
Brennu-Njáls saga 1954. Ed. Einar Ól. Sveinsson. Íslenzk fornrit XII. Reykjavík.
Brot af Þorláks sögu hini elztu. In *Biskupa sögur* 1858–78, I 391–94.
Brot úr miðsögu Guðmundar. In *Biskupa sögur* 1858–78, I 559–618.
Byskupa sǫgur 1938–78. Ed. Jón Helgason. Editiones Arnamagnæanæ A:13:2. Copenhagen.
Byskupa sǫgur. MS Perg. fol. no. 5 in the Royal Library of Stockholm 1950. Ed. Jón Helgason. Corpus codicum Islandicorum medii aevi 19. Copenhagen.
Byskupa sögur 1948. Ed. Guðni Jónsson. 3 vols. Reykjavík.
Byskupa ættir. In *Byskupa sǫgur* 1938–78, 1–12.
DI = *Diplomatarium Islandicum Íslenzkt fornbréfasafn* 1857–1972. Ed. Jón Sigurðsson and Jón Þorkelsson. 16 vols. Copenhagen and Reykjavík.
The First Grammatical Treatise 1972. Ed. Hreinn Benediktsson. University of Iceland Publications in Linguistics I. Reykjavík.
Flateyjarbók 1944–45. Ed. Sigurður Nordal. 4 vols. Reykjavík.
Grettis saga 1936. Ed. Guðni Jónsson. Íslenzk fornrit VII. Reykjavík.
Guðmundar saga A. Guðmundar sögur biskups 1 1983. Ed. Stefán Karlsson. Editiones Arnamagnæanæ B:6. Copenhagen.
Heilagra manna søgur. Fortællinger og legender om hellige mænd og kvinder efter gamle haandskrifter 1877. Ed. C. R. Unger. Oslo.
Heimskringla 1941–1951. Ed. Bjarni Aðalbjarnarson. Íslenzk fornrit XXVI–XXVIII. Reykjavík.
HN = *Historia de antiquitate regum norwagiensium* 1880. Ed. G. Storm. Monumenta Historica Norvegiæ. Latinske kildeskrifter til Norges historie i middelalderen. Oslo.
Homiliu-bók. Isländska homilier efter en handskrift från tolfte århundradet 1872. Ed. Theodor Wisén. Lund.
Hungrvaka. In *Biskupa sögur* II 2002, 1–43.
ÍF = *Íslenzk fornrit* 1933–. Reykjavík.
Islandske Annaler indtil 1578 1888. Ed. Gustav Storm. Det norske historiske Kildeskriftfonds Skrifter 21. Oslo.
Íslendingabók. In *Íslendingabók. Landnámabók* 1968. Ed. Jakob Benediktsson. Íslenzk fornrit I. Reykjavík.
Jarteinabók Þorláks byskups 1199. In *Byskupa sögur* 1948, I 155–91.
Jarteinabók Þorláks byskups in forna. In *Biskupa sögur* II 2002, 101–40. [*Jarteinabók* I]
Jarteinabók Þorláks byskups in yngsta. In *Byskupa sögur* 1948, I 223–49.
Jarteinabók Þorláks byskups önnur 1948. In *Byskupa sögur* 1948, I 193–221.
Jarteinabók Þorláks byskups önnur 2002. In *Biskupa sögur* II 2002, 225–50. [*Jarteinabók* II]

52   Bibliography

Jarteinabók Þorláks frá 1199. In *Biskupa sögur* 1858–78, I 333–56.
Jarteinir úr Þorláks sögu hinni ýngstu. In *Biskupa sögur* 1858–78, I 375–91.
Jóns saga ins helga. Ed. Peter Foote. In *Biskupa sögur* I 2003. Íslenzk fornrit XV, 173–316.
Kristni saga. Ed. Sigurgeir Steingrímsson. In *Biskupa sögur* I 2003. Íslenzk fornrit XV, 1–48.
Landnámabók. In *Íslendingabók. Landnámabók* 1968. Ed. Jakob Benediktsson. Íslenzk fornrit I. Reykjavík.
Latínsk lesbókarbrot um Þorlák. In *Biskupa sögur* 1858–78, I 394–404.
Latínubrot um Þorlák byskup. In *Biskupa sögur* II 2002, 339–64.
Leith, Disney, trans., 1895. *The Story of Bishop Thorlak the Saint. In Stories of the Bishops of Iceland Translated from the Icelandic 'Biskupa Sögur' by the Author of 'The Chorister Brothers*. London.
Líknarbraut. Ed. George S. Tate. In *Skaldic Poetry of the Scandinavian Middle Ages* VII: *Poetry on Christian Subjects*. 1: *The Twelfth and Thirteenth Centuries* 2007. Ed. Margaret Clunies Ross. Turnhout, 228–86.
Norske middelalderdokumenter 1973. Ed. Sverre Bagge et al. Bergen.
Oddaverja þáttr. In *Byskupa sögur* 1948, I 131–54.
Oddaverjaannáll. In *Oddaannálar og Oddaverjaannáll* 2003. Ed. Eiríkur Þormóðsson and Guðrún Ása Grímsdóttir. Stofnun Árna Magnússonar á Íslandi Rit 59. Reykjavík.
Óláfs saga Tryggvasonar en mesta 1958–2000. Ed. Ólafur Halldórsson. Editiones Arnamagnæanæ A:1–3. Copenhagen.
Óláfs saga Tryggvasonar eptir Odd munk Snorrason 2006. Ed. Ólafur Halldórsson. Íslenzk fornrit XXV.
Origines Islandicae. A collection of the more important sagas and other native writings relating to the settlement and early history of Iceland 1905. Ed. and trans. Guðbrandur Vigfússon and F. York Powell. 2 vols. Oxford.
Páls saga byskups. In *Biskupa sögur* II 2002, 295–332.
Postola sögur. Legendariske fortællinger om apostlernes liv. Deres kamp for kristendommens udbredelse samt deres martyrdød 1874. Ed. C. R. Unger. Oslo.
Die religiösen Dichtungen des 11. und 12. Jahrhunderts 1964–70. Ed. F. Maurer. 3 vols. Tübingen.
Saga Guðmundar Arasonar Hólabiskups eptir Arngrím ábóta. In *Biskupa sögur* 1858–78, II 1–187.
Sancti Isidori Hispalensis Sententiarum libri tres 1850. Ed. J.-P. Migne. In *Sancti Isidori Hispalensis episcopi opera omnia*. Patrologia Latina 83. Paris.
Skarðsárbók. Landnámabók Björns Jónssonar á Skarðsá 1958–66. Ed. Jakob Benediktsson. Rit Handritastofnunar Íslands 1. Reykjavík.
Sturlunga saga 1946. Ed. Jón Jóhannesson et al. 2 vols. Reykjavík.
Sverris saga 2007. Ed. Þorleifur Hauksson. Íslenzk fornrit XXX. Reykjavík.
Wolf, Kirsten 1989. 'A translation of the Latin fragments containing the Life and Miracles of St Thorlak along with a Collection of lectiones for Recitation on his Feast-Days'. *Proceedings of the PMR Conference* 14, 261–76.

Þorláks biskups saga hin elzta. In *Biskupa sögur* 1858–78, I 87–124.
Þorláks biskups saga hin yngri. In *Biskupa sögur* 1858–78, I 261–332.
Þorláks saga. In *Biskupa sögur* II 2002.
Þorláks saga byskups. In *Byskupa sögur* 1948, I 33–129.
Þorláks saga byskups C. In *Biskupa sögur* II 2002, 251–85.
Þorláks saga helga. *Elsta gerð Þorláks sögu helga ásamt Jarteinabók og efni úr yngri gerðum sögunnar* 1989. Ed. Ásdís Egilsdóttir. Reykjavík.
Önnur jarteinabók Þorláks. In *Biskupa sögur* 1858–78, I 357–74.

II. SECONDARY LITERATURE

(Includes editions to which reference is made for commentary rather than text)
Ármann Jakobsson 1997. *Í leit að konungi. Konungsmynd íslenskra konungasagna*. Reykjavík.
Ármann Jakobsson 2000. 'Byskupskjör á Íslandi: Stjórnmálaviðhorf byskupasagna og Sturlungu'. *Studia theologica islandica* 14, 171–82.
Ármann Jakobsson 2005. 'Ástin á tímum þjóðveldisins'. In *Miðaldabörn*. Ed. Ármann Jakobsson and Torfi H. Tulinius. Reykjavík, 63–85.
Ármann Jakobsson and Ásdís Egilsdóttir 1998. 'Um Oddaverjaþátt'. *Goðasteinn* 34, 134–43.
Ármann Jakobsson and Ásdís Egilsdóttir 1999. 'Er Oddaverjaþætti treystandi?' *Ný saga* 11, 91–100.
Ásdís Egilsdóttir 1989. 'Formáli'. In *Þorláks saga helga. Elsta gerð Þorláks sögu helga ásamt Jarteinabók og efni úr yngri gerðum sögunnar*, 9–56.
Ásdís Egilsdóttir 1994. 'Mannfræði Höllu biskupsmóður'. In *Sagnaþing helgað Jónasi Kristjánssyni sjötugum 10. apríl 1994*. Ed. Gísli Sigurðsson et al. 2 vols. Reykjavík, I 11–18.
Ásdís Egilsdóttir 2002. 'Formáli'. In *Biskupa sögur* II, v–cli.
Astås, Reidar 1994. 'Om bibelanvendelse i *Þorláks saga byskups*'. *Alvíssmál* 3, 73–96.
Bagge, Sverre 1981. 'Kirkens jurisdiksjon i kristenrettssaker før 1277'. *Historisk tidskrift* 60, 133–59.
Bagge, Sverre 2003. 'Den heroiske tid—kirkereform og kirkekamp 1153–1214'. In *Ecclesia Nidrosiensis 1153–1537. Søkelys på Nidaroskirkens og Nidarosprovinses historie*. Ed. Steinar Imsen. Senter for middelalderstudier, NTNU, Skrifter 15. Trondheim, 51–80.
Baldwin, Marshall W. 1968. *Alexander III and the Twelfth Century*. The Popes through history 3. Glenn Rock.
Bekker-Nielsen, Hans 1965. 'Legender – Helgensagaer'. In *Norrøn Fortællekunst. Kapitler af den norsk-islandske middelalderlitteraturs historie*. Ed. Hans Bekker-Nielsen et al. Copenhagen, 118–26.
Bekker-Nielsen, Hans 1968. 'The Victorines and their influence on Old Norse literature'. In *The Fifth Viking Congress*. Ed. Bjarni Niclasen. Thorshavn, 32–36.
Bekker-Nielsen, Hans 1976. 'Viktorinsk indflydelse'. In *KLNM* XX, 61–63.
Benjamín Kristjánsson 1947. 'Menntun presta á Íslandi fram að siðaskiptum'. *Kirkjuritið* 13:1, 2–31, 140–73, 233–58.

Bibliography

Benjamín Kristjánsson 1958. 'Skálholtsskóli'. In *Skálholtshátíðin 1956. Minning níu alda biskupsdóms á Íslandi*. [Hafnarfjörður], 195–259.

Birkeli, Fridtjov 1973. *Norske steinkors i tidlig middelalder. Et bidrag til belysningen av overgangen fra norrøn religion til kristendom*. Skrifter utgitt av Det Norske Videnskaps-Akademi i Oslo 2. Hist.-filos. klasse. ny serie 10. Oslo.

Birkeli, Fridtjov 1982. *Hva vet vi om kristningen av Norge. Utforskningen av norsk kristendoms- og kirkehistorie fra 900- til 1200-tallet*. Oslo.

Bjarni Aðalbjarnarson 1958. 'Bemærkninger om de eldste bispesagaer'. *Studia Islandica* 17, 27–37.

Bjarni Sigurðsson 1986. *Geschichte und Gegenwartsgestalt des isländischen Kirchenrechts*. Europäische Hochschulschriften 2. Rechtswissenschaft 11:524. Frankfurt am Main.

Björn Þórðarson 1949–1953 [1953]. 'Móðir Jóru biskupsdóttur'. *Saga* 1, 289–346.

Björn Karel Þórólfsson 1956. 'Inngangur'. *Skrár Þjóðskjalasafns* 3. *Biskupsskjalasafn*. Reykjavík, 7–76.

Björn Þorsteinsson 1978. *Íslensk miðaldasaga*. Reykjavík.

Blöndal, Sigfús 1949. 'St. Nikulás og dýrkun hans, sérstaklega á Íslandi'. *Skírnir* 123, 67–97.

Boyer, Régis 1973. 'The Influence of Pope Gregory's *Dialogues* on Old Icelandic Literature'. In *Proceedings of the First International Saga Conference*. Ed. Peter Foote et al. London, 1–27.

Bugge, Alexander 1916. 'Kirke og stat i Norge 1152–64'. *Historisk tidskrift* 24, 160–212.

Bull, Edvard 1915. *Den pavelige legat Stephanus i Norge (1163)*. Norske videnskaps-akademi i Oslo. Historisk-filosofisk klasse 1915:2. Oslo.

Bynum, Caroline Walker 1979. *Docere Verbo et Exemplo. An Aspect of Twelfth-Century Spirituality*. Harvard theological studies 31. Missoula.

Bynum, Caroline Walker 1982. 'The Spirituality of the Regular Canons in the Twelfth Century'. In *Jesus as a Mother. Studies in the Spirituality of the High Middle Ages*. Berkeley, 22–58.

Carlsson, Thorsten 1972. 'Norrön legendforskning—en kort presentation'. *Scripta Islandica* 23, 31–58.

Collings, Lucy 1969. *The Codex Scardensis. Studies in Icelandic Hagiography*. PhD dissertation, Cornell University.

Cormack, Margaret 1994. *The Saints in Iceland. Their Veneration from the Conversion to 1400*. Subsidia hagiographica 78. Brussels.

Cormack, Margaret 2005. 'Christian Biography'. In *A Companion to Old Norse-Icelandic Literature and Culture*. Ed. R. McTurk. Oxford, 27–42.

Coviaux, Stéphane 2006. 'Les évêques norvégiens et les idées politiques d'Occident au XIIe siècle'. *Médiévales* 50, 29–46.

DuBois, Thomas, ed., 2008. *Sanctity in the North. Saints, Lives, and Cults in Medieval Scandinavia*. Toronto Old Norse-Icelandic Series 4. Toronto.

Einar Arnórsson 1930. 'Alþingi árið 1000'. *Skírnir* 104, 68–106.

Einar Ól. Sveinsson 1936. 'Jarteiknir'. *Skírnir* 110, 23–48.

Einar Ól. Sveinsson 1954. 'Formáli'. In *Páls saga biskups*. Ed. Einar Ól. Sveinsson. Reykjavík, 3–13.
Eldjárn, Kristján 1988. 'Gröf Páls biskups Jónssonar'. In *Skálholt. Fornleifarannsóknir 1954–1958*. Ed. Kristján Eldjárn et al. Reykjavík, 147–58.
Ferrulo, Stephen C. 1985. *The Origins of the University. The schools of Paris and their Critics, 1100–1215*. Stanford.
Finnur Jónsson 1907. 'Tilnavne i den islandske oldlitteratur'. *Årbøger for nordisk oldkyndighed og historie* 22, 161–381.
Finnur Jónsson 1920–24. *Den oldnorske og oldislandske litteraturs historie*. 2nd ed. 3 vols. Copenhagen.
Finucane, Ronald C. 1977. *Miracles and Pilgrims. Popular Beliefs in Medieval England*. Totowa.
Foote, Peter 1962. 'Introduction'. In *Lives of Saints. Perg. Fol. Nr. 2 in the Royal Library, Stockholm*. Ed. Peter Foote. Early Icelandic Manuscripts in Facsimile 4. Copenhagen, 7–29.
Foote, Peter 1975. 'Aachen. Lund. Hólar'. In *Les relations littéraires Franco-Scandinaves au moyen âge*. Les congrès et colloques de l'université de Liège 73. Actes du Colloque de Liège. Paris, 53–73.
Foote, Peter 2003. 'Formáli. III: Jóns saga helga'. In *Biskupa sögur* I. Íslenzk fornrit XV, ccxiii–cccxxi.
Gad, Tue 1961. *Legenden i dansk middelalder*. Copenhagen.
Gad, Tue 1967. 'Nicolaus af Myra'. In *KLNM* XII, 288–91.
Gjerløw, Lilli 1961. 'Hallvard'. In *KLNM* VI, 63–66.
Gjerløw, Lilli 1965. 'Lectionarium'. In *KLNM* X, 390–92.
Gjerløw, Lilli 1970. 'Seljumannamessa'. In *KLNM* XV, 118–21.
Gottskálk Þór Jensson 2003. 'The Latin Fragments of *Þorláks saga helga* and their Classical Context'. In *Scandinavia and the Christian Europe in the Middle Ages. Papers of the 12th International Saga Conference, Bonn, Germany. 28th July–2nd August 2003*. Ed. R. Simek and J. Meurer. Bonn, 257–67.
Gottskálk Þór Jensson 2004. 'The Lost Latin Literature of Medieval Iceland: The Fragments of the *Vita Sancti Thorlaci* and other Evidence'. *Symbolae Osolenses* 79, 150–70.
Gottskálk Þór Jensson 2009. 'Nokkrar athugasemdir um latínubrotin úr Vita sancti Thorlaci episcopi et confessoris'. In *Pulvis Olympicus. Afmælisrit tileinkað Sigurði Péturssyni*. Ed. Jón Ma. Ásgeirsson et al. Reykjavík, 97–109.
Grønlie, Siân 2005. 'Kristni saga and Medieval Conversion History'. *Gripla* XVI, 137–59.
Guðbrandur Vigfússon 1858. 'Formáli'. In *Biskupa sögur* 1858–78, I v–xc.
Guðrún Ása Grímsdóttir 1982. 'Um afskipti erkibiskupa af íslenzkum málefnum á 12. og 13. öld'. *Saga* 20, 28–62.
Guðrún Ása Grímsdóttir 1998. 'Formáli'. In *Biskupa sögur* III. Íslenzk fornrit XVII, v–cxxxvii.
Gunnar F. Guðmundsson 2000. *Íslenskt samfélag og Rómakirkja*. Kristni á Íslandi 2. Reykjavík.

Halldór Hermannsson 1958. *The Hólar Cato. An Icelandic Schoolbook of the Seventeenth Century*. Islandica 39. Ithaca.

Hannes Þorsteinsson 1912. 'Nokkrar athuganir um íslenzkar bókmentir á 12. og 13. öld'. *Skírnir* 86, 126–48.

Heffernan, Thomas J. 1988. *Sacred Biography. Saints and their Biographers in the Middle Ages*. New York.

Heffernan, Thomas J. 2003. 'Christian Biography: Foundations to Maturity'. In *Historiography in the Middle Ages*. Ed. D. M. Deliyannis. Leiden, 115–54.

Heinzelmann, Martin 1979. *Translationsberichte und andere Quellen des Reliquienkultes*. Typologie des sources du Moyen Âge occidental 33. Turnhout.

Helander, Sven 1957. 'Breviarium'. In *KLNM* II, 236–38.

Helgi Guðmundsson 2003. 'Þorláks saga biskups og Isidor'. *Gripla* XIV, 237–38.

Helgi Þorláksson 1989. *Gamlar götur og goðavald. Um fornar leiðir og völd Oddaverja í Rangárþingi*. Ritsafn Sagnfræðistofnunar 25. Reykjavík.

Helle, Knut 1974. *Norge blir en stat 1130–1319*. Handbok i Norges historie 3. 2nd ed. Bergen.

Helle, Knut 1981. 'Norway in the High Middle Ages: Recent Views on the Structure of Society'. *Scandinavia Journal of History* 6, 161–89.

Hjalti Hugason 2000. *Frumkristni og upphaf kirkju*. Kristni á Íslandi 1. Reykjavík.

Holtsmark, Anne 1938. 'Introduction'. In *A Book of Miracles. MS No. 645 4to of the Arna-Magnæan Collection in the University Library of Copenhagen*. Corpus codicium Islandicorum medii aevii 12. Copenhagen, 5–27.

Holtzmann, Walther 1938. 'Krone und Kirche in Norwegen im 12. Jahrhundert (Englische Analekten III)'. *Deutsches Archiv für Geschichte des Mittelalters* 2, 341–400.

Jakob Benediktsson 1969. 'Brot úr Þorlákslesi'. In *Afmælisrit Jóns Helgasonar 30. júní 1969*. Ed. Jakob Benediktsson et al. Reykjavík, 98–108.

Jakob Benediktsson 1970. 'Skole, Island'. In *KLNM* XV, 640.

Janus Jónsson 1887. 'Um klaustrin á Íslandi'. *Tímarit hins íslenzka bókmenntafélags* 8, 174–265.

Johnsen, Arne Odd 1945. 'Om St Victorsklostret og nordmennene'. *Norsk Historisk tidsskrift* 33, 405–32.

Johnsen, Arne Odd 1951a. *Om erkebiskop Øysteins eksil 1180–1183*. Det kongelige Norske Videnskabers Selskabs Skrifter 1950:5. Trondheim.

Johnsen, Arne Odd 1951b. 'Les relations intellectuelles entre la France et la Norvège (1150–1214)'. *Le Moyen Âge* 57, 247–68.

Johnsen, Arne Odd 1967. *On the background for the establishment of the Norwegian church province. Some new viewpoints*. Avhandlinger utgitt af Det Norske Videnskaps-Akademi i Oslo 2. Hist.-Filos. klasse. ny serie 11. Oslo.

Jón Böðvarsson 1968. 'Munur eldri og yngri gerðar Þorláks sögu'. *Saga* 6, 81–94.

Jón Thor Haraldsson 1988. *Ósigur Oddaverja*. Ritsafn Sagnfræðistofnunar Háskóla Íslands 22. Reykjavík.

Jón Helgason 1934. *Norrøn litteraturhistorie*. Copenhagen.

Jón Helgason 1950. 'Introduction'. In *Byskupa sǫgur. MS Perg. fol. no. 5 in the Royal Library of Stockholm*, 7–22.

Jón Helgason 1976. 'Þorláks saga'. In *KLNM* XX, 388–91.
Jón Jóhannesson 1952. 'Tímatal Gerlands í íslenzkum ritum frá þjóðveldisöld'. *Skírnir* 126, 76–93.
Jón Jóhannesson 1956–58. *Íslendingasaga*. 2 vols. Reykjavík.
Jón Viðar Sigurðsson 2006. 'Samskipti íslenskra biskupa við útlenda yfirboðara á öldum áður'. In *Saga biskupsstólanna. Skálholt 950 ára – 2006 – Hólar 900 ára*. Ed. Gunnar Kristjánsson. Akureyri, 490–515.
Jón Stefánsson 1950. 'Rúðólf of Bœ and Rudolf of Rouen'. *Saga-Book* XIII, 174–82.
Jónas Kristjánsson 1975. 'Íslenzk bókmenntasaga'. In *Saga Íslands* II. Ed. Sigurður Líndal. Reykjavík, 145–258.
Joys, Charles 1948. *Biskop og konge. Bispevalg i Norge 1000-1350*. Oslo.
Jørgensen, Jørgen Højgaard 1982. 'Hagiography and the Icelandic bishop sagas'. *Pertitia* I, 1–16.
Kemp, Eric Waldram 1948. *Canonization and Authority in the Western Church*. Oxford Historical Series. London.
Kirby, Ian J. 1976–80. *Biblical Quotation in Old Icelandic-Norwegian Religious Literature*. Stofnun Árna Magnússonar á Íslandi. Rit 9–10. 2 vols. Reykjavík.
Kirby, Ian J. 1993. 'Christian Prose. 2. West Norse'. In *Medieval Scandinavia. An Encyclopedia*. Ed. Phillip Pulsiano. New York, 79–80.
KLNM = Kulturhistorisk leksikon for nordisk middelalder fra vikingtid til reformationstid I–XXII 1956–78.
Köhne, Roland 1972. 'Bischof Ísleifr Gizurarson, ein berühmter Schüler des Stifts Herford. Kirchliche Verbindungen zwischen Deutschland und Island im 11. Jahrhundert'. *Jahresbericht des Historischen Vereins der Grafschaft Ravensberg* 67, 1–38.
Köhne, Roland 1974. 'Herford und Island'. *Island. Deutsch-isländisches Jahrbuch* 7, 21–23.
Köhne, Roland 1987. 'Wirklichkeit und Fiktion in den mittelalterlichen Nachrichten über Ísleif Gizurarson'. *Skandinavistik* 17:1, 24–30.
Kolsrud, Oluf 1958. *Norges kyrkjesoga*. I: *Millomalderen*. Oslo.
Kratz, Henry 1993. 'Saints' Lives. 2. Iceland and Norway'. In *Medieval Scandinavia. An Encyclopedia*. Ed. Phillip Pulsiano. New York, 562–64.
Kratz, Henry 1994. 'Thorlákr's Miracles'. In *Samtíðarsögur. Níunda alþjóðlega fornsagnaþingið. Akureyri 31.7. – 6.8.1994. Forprent*. Reykjavík, 480–94.
Kuhn, Hans 1994. 'The Emergence of a Saint's Cult as Witnessed by the *Jarteinabækr Þorláks byskups*'. In *Samtíðarsögur. Níunda alþjóðlega fornsagnaþingið. Akureyri 31.7. – 6.8.1994. Forprent*. Reykjavík. 506–19.
Laugesen, Anker Teilgård 1959. *Syv – ni – tolv. Nogle iagttagelser over typiske tal i litteraturen*. Studier fra Sprog- og Oldtidsforskning 237. Copenhagen.
Líndal, Sigurður 1974. 'Upphaf kristni og kirkju'. In *Saga Íslands* 1. Ed. Sigurður Líndal. Reykjavík, 225–88.
Ljungberg, Helge 1938. *Den nordiska religionen och kristendomen. Studier över det nordiska religionsskiftet under vikingtiden*. Nordiska texter och undersökningar 11. Stockholm.

Loth, Agnete 1984. 'Indledning'. In *Den gamle jærtegnsbog om biskop Thorlak*. [Odense], 9–22.
Lundén, Tryggve 1950. 'Om de medeltida svenska mirakelsamlingarna'. *Kyrkohistorisk Årsskrift* 50, 33–60.
Magerøy, Hallvard 1961. 'Helgensoger'. In *KLNM* VI, 350–53.
Magnús Már Lárusson 1956 [1967]. 'Biskupskjör á Íslandi'. *Andvari* 81, 87–100.. Reprinted in *Fróðleikspættir og sögubrot*. [Hafnarfjörður], 50–61.
Magnús Már Lárusson 1959a. 'Um hina ermsku biskupa'. *Skírnir* 133, 81–94.
Magnús Már Lárusson 1959b. 'Fostring'. In *KLNM* IV, 544–45.
Magnús Már Lárusson 1960–1963 [1962]. 'Sct. Magnus Orcadensis Comes'. *Saga* 3, 470–503.
Magnús Már Lárusson 1962. 'Jón helgi Ögmundarson'. In *KLNM* VII, 608–12.
Magnús Már Lárusson 1963a. 'Katedralskola, Island'. In *KLNM* VIII, 353–54.
Magnús Már Lárusson 1963b. 'Kloster'. In *KLNM* VIII, 544–46.
Magnús Már Lárusson 1968. 'Privatkirke'. In *KLNM* XIII, 462–67.
Magnús Stefánsson 1975. 'Kirkjuvald eflist'. In *Saga Íslands* II. Ed. Sigurður Líndal. Reykjavík, 55–144.
Magnús Stefánsson 1978. 'Frá goðakirkju til biskupakirkju'. In *Saga Íslands* III. Ed. Sigurður Líndal. Reykjavík, 109–257.
Magnús Stefánsson 2000. *Staðir og staðamál. Studier i islandske egenkirkelige og benficialrettslige forhold i middelalderen* 1. Historisk Institutts skriftserie 4. Bergen.
Magnús Stefánsson 2002. 'Um staði og staðamál'. *Saga* 40, 139–66.
Magnús Stefánsson 2005. 'De islandske stadenes egenart og eldste historie'. In *Church Centres. Church Centres in Iceland from the 11th to the 13th Century and their Parallels in other Countries*. Ed. Helgi Þorláksson. Reykholt, 121–29.
Maurer, Konrad von 1855–56. *Die Bekehrung des Norwegischen Stammes zum Christenthume in ihrem geschichtlichen Verlaufe quellenmäßig geschildert*. 2 vols. Munich.
Meisen, Karl 1931. *Nikolauskult und Nikolausbrauch im Abendlande. Eine kulturgeographisch-volkskundliche Untersuchung*. Forschungen zur Volkskunde 9:12. Quellen und Abhandlungen zur mittelrheinischen Kirchengeschichte 41. Düsseldorf.
Melsted, Bogi Th. 1903–30. *Íslendinga saga* 1. *Fundur Íslands og landnám*. 2. *Ísland sjálfstætt ríki. Þjóðveldið*. 3. *Annað tímabil. Þroskatíð kristninnar 1030–1200*. Copenhagen.
Melsteð, Bogi Th. 1912–14. 'Ferðir, siglingar og samgöngur milli Íslands og annarra landa á dögum þjóðveldisins'. *Safn til sögu Íslands og íslenzkra bókmenta að fornu og nýju* 4.
Mogk, Eugen 1904. *Geschichte der Norwegisch-Isländischen Literatur*. 2nd ed. Strasbourg.
Moore, Robert Ian 2000. *The First European Revolution. c.970–c.1215. The Making of Europe*. Oxford.
Nordal, Sigurður 1933. 'Formáli'. In *Egils saga Skalla-Grímssonar*. Íslenzk fornrit II. Reykjavík, v–cv.

Nordal, Sigurður 1952. 'Sagalitteraturen'. In *Litteraturhistoria* B. *Norge og Island*. Nordisk Kultur 8. Stockholm, 180–273.

Ólafía Einarsdóttir 1964. *Studier i kronologisk metode i tidlig islandsk historieskrivning*. Bibliotheca historica Lundensis 13. Lund.

Ólafur Halldórsson 1985. 'Formáli'. In *Eiríks saga rauða. Texti Skálholtsbókar*. Íslenzk fornrit IV (Viðauki), 333–99.

Ordbog = *Ordbog over det norrøne prosasprog* 1–3 1989–. Ed. Helle Degnbol et al. Copenhagen.

Orri Vésteinsson 2000. *The Christianization of Iceland. Priests, Power, and Social Change 1000–1300*. Oxford.

Orrman, Eljas 2003. 'Church and Society'. In *The Cambridge History of Scandinavia* 1. *Prehistory to 1520*. Ed. Knut Helle. Cambridge, 421–62.

Owen, Dorothy M. 1971. *Church and Society in Medieval Lincolnshire*. History of Lincolnshire 5. Lincoln.

Paasche, Fredrik 1914. *Kristendom og kvad. En studie i norrøn middelalder*. Oslo.

Paasche, Fredrik 1958. *Møtet mellom hedendom og kristendom i Norden*. Olaus Petri-forelesninger ved Uppsala universitet våren 1941. Oslo.

Piebenga, Gryt Anne 1993. 'Collections of Miracles'. In *Medieval Scandinavia. An Encyclopedia*. Ed. Phillip Pulsiano. New York, 413–14.

Samuelson, David Robert 1977. *The operation of the bishop's legend in early medieval England and Iceland*. PhD dissertation, University of Michigan.

Sanmark, Alexandra 2004. *Power and Conversion. A Comparative Study of Christianization in Scandinavia*. Occasional Papers in Archaeology 34. Uppsala.

Schlafke, Jakob 1960. 'Das Recht der Bischöfe in causis sanctorum bis zum Jahre 1234'. In *Die Kirche und ihre Ämter und Stände. Festgabe seiner Eminenz dem hochwürdigsten Herrn Joseph Kardinal Frings. Erzbischof von Köln zum goldenen Priesterjubiläum am 10. August 1960 dargeboten*. Ed. W. Corsten et al. Cologne, 417–33.

Schmale, Franz-Josef 1961. *Studien zum Schisma des Jahres 1130*. Forschungen zur kirchlichen Rechtsgeschichte und zum Kirchenrecht 3. Cologne.

Seip, Didrik Arup 1963. 'Jærtegnsamlinger'. In *KLNM* VIII, 65–68.

Sicard, Patrice 1991. *Hugues de Saint-Victor et son école*. Turnhout.

Skovgaard-Petersen, Inge 1960. 'Islandsk egenkirkevæsen'. *Scandia* 26, 230–96.

Skre, Dagfinn 1998. 'Missionary Activities in Early Medieval Norway. Strategy, Organization and the Course of Events'. *Scandinavian Journal of History* 23, 1–19.

Stancliffe, Clare 1983. *St. Martin and his Hagiographer. History and Miracle in Sulpicius Severus*. Oxford historical monographs. Oxford.

Steinunn Kristjánsdóttir 2007. 'Kristnitakan. Áhrif tilviljanakennds og skipulegs trúboðs'. *Saga* 45:1, 113–30.

Sveinbjörn Rafnsson 1977. 'Um kristniboðsþættina'. *Gripla* II, 19–31.

Sveinbjörn Rafnsson 1982a. 'Skriftaboð Þorláks biskups'. *Gripla* V, 77–114.

Sveinbjörn Rafnsson 1982b. 'Þorláksskriftir og hjúskapur á 12. og 13. öld'. *Saga* 20, 114–29.

Sveinbjörn Rafnsson 1985. 'The Penitential of St. Þorlákur in its Icelandic context'. *Bulletin of Medieval Canon Law*. New Series 15, 19–30.

Sveinbjörn Rafnsson 1993. *Páll Jónsson Skálholtsbiskup. Nokkrar athuganir á sögu hans og kirkjustjórn*. Ritsafn Sagnfræðistofnunar 33. Reykjavík.

Sverrir Tómasson 1982. 'Íslenskar Nikulás sögur'. In *Helgastaðabók. Nikulás saga. Perg. 4to Nr. 16 Konungsbókhlöðu í Stokkhólmi*. Manuscripta Islandica medii aevi 2. Reykjavík, 11–41.

Sverrir Tómasson 1988. *Formálar íslenskra sagnaritara á miðöldum. Rannsókn bókmenntahefðar*. Stofnun Árna Magnússonar á Íslandi. Rit 33. Reykjavík.

Sverrir Tómasson 1992. 'Kristnar trúarbókmenntir í óbundnu máli'. In *Íslensk bókmenntasaga* 1. Ed. Vésteinn Ólason. Reykjavík, 419–79.

Sverrir Tómasson 1993. 'Trúarbókmenntir í lausu máli á síðmiðöld'. In *Íslensk bókmenntasaga* 2. Ed. Vésteinn Ólason. Reykjavík, 247–81.

Sverrir Tómasson 2007. 'Helgisögur og helgisagnaritun'. In *Heilagra karla sögur*. Ed. Sverrir Tómasson et al. Íslensk trúarrit 3. Reykjavík, xxi–lx.

Turville-Petre, Gabriel 1953. *Origins of Icelandic Literature*. Oxford.

Vauchez, André 1988. *La sainteté en Occident aux derniers siècles du Moyen Âge. D'après les procès de canonisation et les documents hagiographiques*. Bibliothèque des écoles françaises d'Athènes et de Rome 241. Rome.

Walter, Ernst 1971. 'Die lateinische Sprache und Literatur auf Island und in Norwegen bis zum Beginn des 13. Jahrhunderts. Ein Orientierungsversuch'. *Nordeuropa Studien* 4, 195–230.

Ward, Benedicta 1982. *Miracles and the Medieval Mind. Theory, Record, and Event, 1000–1215*. London.

Weinstein, Donald and Rudolph M. Bell 1982. *Saints and Society. The Two Worlds and Western Christendom, 1000–1700*. Chicago.

Whaley, Diana 1994. 'Miracles in the *Biskupa sögur*: Icelandic Variations on an International Theme'. In *Samtíðarsögur. Níunda alþjóðlega fornsagnaþingið. Akureyri 31.7. – 6.8.1994. Forprent* 1. Reykjavík, 847–62.

Widding, Ole 1961a. 'Kilderne til den norrøne Nicolaus saga'. *Opuscula* 2:1. Bibliotheca Arnamagnæana 25:1, 17–27.

Widding, Ole 1961b. 'AM 655 4to. fragment III. Et brudstykke af Nicolaus saga'. *Opuscula* 2:1. Bibliotheca Arnamagnæana 25:1, 27–33.

Widding, Ole 1965. 'Jærtegn og Maríu saga. Eventyr'. In *Norrøn Fortællekunst. Kapitler af den norsk-islandske middelalderlitteraturs historie*. Ed. Hans Bekker-Nielsen et al. Copenhagen, 127–36.

Widding, Ole, Hans Bekker-Nielsen and L. K. Shook 1963. 'The Lives of theSaints in Old Norse Prose. A Handlist'. *Mediaeval Studies* 23, 294–337.

Widding, Ole and Hans Bekker-Nielsen 1965. 'Legende. Norge og Island'. In *KLNM* X, 421–23.

Wolf, Kirsten 1993a. 'Legenda'. In *Medieval Scandinavia. An Encyclopedia*. Ed. Phillip Pulsiano. New York, 388–89.

Wolf, Kirsten 1993b. 'Postola sögur'. In *Medieval Scandinavia. An Encyclopedia*. Ed. Phillip Pulsiano. New York, 511–12.

Wolf, Kirsten 2003. 'Inngangur'. In *Heilagra meyja sögur*. Ed. Kirsten Wolf. Íslensk trúarrit 1. Reykjavík, 9–67.

Wolf, Kirsten 2008. 'Pride and Politics in Late-Twelfth-Century Iceland: The Sanctity of Bishop Þorlákr Þórhallsson'. In *Sanctity in the North. Saints, Lives, and Cults in Medieval Scandinavia*. Ed. Thomas A. DuBois. Toronto Old Norse-Icelandic Series 4. Toronto, 241–70.

Þorleifur Hauksson and Þórir Óskarsson 1994. *Íslensk stílfræði*. Reykjavík.

Þorleifur Hauksson 2007. 'Formáli'. In *Sverris saga*. Íslenzk fornrit XXX. Reykjavík, v–xc.

INDEX OF PERSONAL NAMES

Agnes, saint 16
Alexander III (d. 1181), pope 11
Ambrose, saint 16
Anacletus (d. 1138), pope 1
Árni, worthy man 25
Bjarnheðinn (d. 1173), monk 5, 7
Bjǫrn Gilsson (d. 1162), bishop of Hólar 3
Brandr Sæmundarson (d. 1201), bishop of Hólar 20, 23, 31
Cecilia, saint 16
Christ 2, 6, 13, 21
David, prophet 1, 2, 3, 8, 11, 13, 14, 16, 21
Eiríkr Ívarsson (d. 1213), bishop and later archbishop of Norway 11, 23
Erlingr the crooked (d. 1179), Norwegian earl 11
Eyjólfr Sæmundarson (d. 1158), priest and magnate 2
Eysteinn Erlendsson (d. 1188), archbishop of Norway 9, 11
Eyvǫr, Þorlákr's sister 4
Gizurr Hallsson (d. 1206), Icelandic magnate and lawspeaker 10, 19–23
God 1, 4–9, 11, 13–26, 31, 32
Gregory the Great (d. 604), pope and saint 18
Guðmundr Arason (d. 1237), bishop of Hólar 31
Guðmundr gríss Ámundason (d. 1210), chieftain 24
Guðmundr Bjálfason (d. 1197), abbot in Þykkvabœr 16
Halla, Þorlákr's mother 1, 7
Hallr Gizurarson (d. 1230), Icelandic magnate and lawspeaker 31
Haraldr Gilchrist (d. 1136), king of Norway 1
Isidore (d. 636), saint 2
James, apostle 14
John, apostle 14
Jón Ljótsson (Loptsson), abbot in Þykkvabœr 24
Jón Loptsson (d. 1197), Icelandic magnate 10
Karl Jónsson (d. 1212), abbot at Þingeyrar 22
Klœngr Þorsteinsson (d. 1176), bishop of Skálaholt 7, 9–10
Laurence, saint 12
Luke, evangelist 6
Magnús Einarsson (d. 1148), bishop of Skálaholt 2–3
Magnús Erlingsson (d. 1184), king of Norway 11
Magnús Gizurarson (d. 1237), bishop of Skálaholt 26, 31
Magnús Sigurðarson (d. 1139), king of Norway 1
Martin, saint 19
Mary, virgin and saint 18
Nicholas, saint 16
Ormr Eyjólfsson, chaplain 21, 23
Ormr Jónsson (d. 1218), Icelandic magnate 25, 31

Paul, apostle 2, 8, 10–12, 14–15, 18
Páll (d. 1194), bishop of Bergen 11
Páll Jónsson (d. 1211), bishop of Skálaholt 4, 19–21, 23–25, 28, 31–32
Páll Solvason (d. 1185), priest at Reykjaholt 9, 19
Peter, apostle 11, 24
Ragnheiðr Þórhallsdóttir, Þorlákr's sister 4
Sighvatr, noble man 24
Solomon the Wise, Biblical king 1, 18
Sveinn, farmer 23
Sverrir Sigurðarson (d. 1202), king of Norway 11
Sæmundr Jónsson (d. 1222), Icelandic magnate 31
Timothy, saint 12
Titus, saint 11
Tjörvi, leper 24
Torfi, priest 25
Unas, sick man 24
Uni, cripple 31
Vitus, saint 25
Þorkell Geirason (d. 1187), patron of Þorlákr 6, 9–10, 16, 21
Þorlákr Þórhallsson (d. 1193), saint and bishop of Skálaholt 1–32
Þorlákr Runólfsson (d. 1133), bishop of Skálaholt 1
Þorleifr Þorleiksson (d. 1200), from Hítardalr 31
Þorsteinn (Jónsson), young nobleman 31
Þorsteinn Skeggjason, goldsmith 32
Þorvaldr lundi, priest 23
Þorvaldr Gizurarson (d. 1235) 19, 31
Þórðr, noble priest 25
Þórhallr, Þorlákr's father 1
Ǫgmundr Kálfsson (d. 1187), abbot at Helgafell 9

INDEX OF PLACE NAMES

Austfirðir 24
Bergen 11
Caithness 32
Denmark 32
England 3, 32
English Channel 28
Faroe Islands 28, 32
Fljótshlíð, region 1
Gautland (Götland) 32
Gotland 32
Greenland 32
Háfr, farm 5
Hítardalr, farm 31
Hlíðarendi, farm in Fljótshlíð 1
Hólar, see 31
Holtavatn, lake 27
Iceland 1, 3, 4, 6, 8, 10, 11, 22, 23, 27
Kirkjubœr, at Síða, farm 5–7
Lincoln, cathedral town in England 3
Norway 1, 10, 11, 32
Oddi, farm 2
Orkney 28, 32
Paris 3
Reykjaholt, farm 19, 28
Scotland 32
Shetland 32
Síða, region 5
Skálaholt, see 3, 10, 12, 13, 16, 19, 22–25, 31, 32
Stafangr (Stavanger), town in Norway 11
Sweden 32
Vatnsdalr, valley 22
Ver, region, *see* Þykkvabœr
Vestfirðir 30
Vestmannaeyjar 27
Þrándheimr (Trondheim), town in Norway 11
Þykkvabœr, at Ver, farm 6, 7, 16